WHY ABRAHAM?

WHY ABRAHAM?
Genesis and the Qualifications of the Chosen People

Jeffrey M. Jaffe

gefen
publishing house בית הוצאה לאור
JERUSALEM • NEW YORK   Est. 1981

Editor: Kezia Raffel Pride
Cover Design: Leah Ben Avraham/ Noonim Graphics
Typesetting: Optume Technologies

ISBN: 978-965-7801-44-4

1 3 5 7 9 8 6 4 2

Gefen Publishing House Ltd.
6 Hatzvi Street
Jerusalem 9438614
Israel
972-2-538-0247
orders@gefenpublishing.com

Gefen Books
c/o Baker & Taylor Publisher Services
30 Amberwood Parkway
Ashland, Ohio 44805
516-593-1234
orders@gefenpublishing.com

www.gefenpublishing.com
Printed in Israel

Library of Congress Control Number: 2024931743

Contents

Preface...vii

Acknowledgments ix

Introduction   The Chosen People 1

Chapter 1   A Worthy Progenitor...................................... 11

Chapter 2   Abraham's Ten Tests.. 27

Chapter 3   More on the Chosen People 39

Chapter 4   Sarah and the Matriarchs................................ 57

Chapter 5   Explaining Abraham's Apparent Failings........ 67

Chapter 6   Abraham among the Canaanites...................... 93

Chapter 7   The Second Generation – Isaac and Rebecca.... 103

Chapter 8   The Blessings.. 123

Chapter 9   Rebecca's Centrality....................................... 133

Chapter 10   The Third Generation – Jacob......................... 139

Afterword   Takeaways 151

Appendix 1   Analysis of the Vignettes 155

Appendix 2   The Ladder of Tests and Blessings 163

Appendix 3   Explanation of Key Vignettes 167

Preface

A major theme of the book of Genesis is the genealogy of the Jewish people. Starting with Genesis chapter 11, which introduces Abraham, the remaining forty-one chapters are all about the life of Abraham, his children, grandchildren, and great-grandchildren. Evidently the purpose is to introduce the nation that will be freed from slavery and stand at Mount Sinai to receive the Ten Commandments. This nation will have the unique and difficult 613 mitzvot (commandments) to perform, as part of their covenant with God.

The story of that nation could be told in many ways. There must be a purpose to the particular narrative and set of vignettes provided in Genesis. It stands to reason that the purpose of Genesis is to explain and justify why the Patriarchs and the nation of their descendants were worthy of this historical role. While that seems reasonable, it can sometimes be difficult to see how the vignettes in Genesis support the worthiness of the nation.

Accordingly, the purpose of this book is to explain based on the language of Genesis that the first biblical book indeed is precise in explaining the worthiness of the Patriarchs. But along the way, we will need to address several confusing questions and topics:

- Why did God decide to have a Chosen People at all? Did He always plan on having such a nation?
- What were the special qualifications of the Patriarchs (particularly Abraham, the first Patriarch) that enabled them to be progenitors of the Chosen People?
- Why did God choose the particular timing that He did to form a covenant with one nation?
- Why are all the children of Jacob included in the covenant – even those who sinned – whereas some of the children of Abraham and Isaac are not included?
- What is the background of the love that Isaac had for his sinful son Esau, and why was he so intent on providing him with extraordinary blessings?

- In this patriarchal description, what was the role of the Matriarchs?
- We will explain some of the detours in the text. There are long sections (e.g., the chapter 14 war) that seem irrelevant to the main topic of Genesis yet occupy a significant amount of space. What is the cosmic importance of these vignettes?
- We will explain some of the behaviors of the Patriarchs that may appear to be less than praiseworthy.

All of these questions tend to be meta-questions about the purpose of the Genesis text. Whereas most commentaries on Genesis focus on the meanings and lessons of particular words and phrases, our focus is to address the big-picture questions about the Genesis narrative.

Please note that when we reference a verse in Genesis, we will not repeat the book name each time, so all unattributed verse numbers may be assumed to refer to the book of Genesis.

In 17:5 and 17:15, God changes Abraham's name from his birth name of Abram to Abraham and changes Sarai's name to Sarah. In this book, we will consistently use the names Abraham and Sarah throughout, even when referring to their earlier years.

Acknowledgments

A major effort such as writing a book requires a confidante, sounding board, and (sometimes) a critic. I would like to thank my wife, Esther Jaffe, who filled all those roles and spent hours reviewing and critiquing my early manuscripts.

I also appreciate and thank the team at Gefen – including Senior Editor Kezia Raffel Pride and Publisher Ilan Greenfield, for tremendous efforts in reviewing the book – and also for popularizing my previous book *Genesis: A Torah for All Nations*, which was also published by Gefen.

Introduction

The Chosen People

Beneath the questions posed in the preface lies the fundamental problem of what it means for the Jews to be chosen.

The first question that presents itself in today's egalitarian world is why *any* nation would be designated by God to be chosen. Aren't we all equal? Is this terminology even acceptable? To address this underlying question, we must first explain what qualified the Patriarchs to become our nation's founders. Once we understand those qualifications, we will be able to understand their mission and fathom God's design in having selected a Chosen People. Whatever the reason, it is undeniable that in the Five Books of Moses, the Jews are designated as God's Chosen People. God establishes various covenants with Abraham, guaranteeing that his descendants will reap rewards, most notably ownership of the Land of Israel.

Further, many of the 613 commandments given to the Jews implicitly flow from their status as the Chosen People. No one proposes that any nation other than the Jews be required to eat kosher (Leviticus chapter 11) or prohibited from starting a fire on the Sabbath (Exodus 35:3).

Further, the Torah explicitly designates the Jews as the Chosen People. Deuteronomy 7:6 states, "The Lord your God has chosen you to be His own treasure, out of all of the peoples that are upon the face of the earth." Deuteronomy 14:1 describes the Jews as "children to God." Mishnah *Avot* (*Pirkei Avot* or Ethics of the Fathers) 3:14 explains that the Jews' status as metaphorical sons to God is due to God's love for the Jewish people. And Exodus 19:5 similarly records, "you shall be My own treasure from among all peoples."

While we have not yet explained the role of the Chosen People, it is clear that the descendants of Abraham are thus labeled. It is against this backdrop that we can begin to properly understand the Book of Genesis, much of whose purpose is to explain how and why the Jews were chosen.

What is more, the Torah goes beyond designating the children of Abraham as having been chosen. Abraham had many children, and the Torah needs to explain which ones received the inheritance. The Torah also must indicate why Abraham, Isaac, Jacob, and their descendants were deserving of carrying on this legacy. The Book of Genesis thus provides a documentary of the key events that forged the Jewish people.

The Qualifications of the Chosen People

Against this backdrop, we might expect to find in Genesis a narrative that explains why Abraham and his family are deserving. The Patriarchs and Matriarchs might be presented as heroic leaders, men and women of great deeds. Verse after verse would convey important ethical teachings that account for their destiny. In short, we would expect the Torah to explain why the Jewish people were chosen.

Indeed, this expectation is realized in later traditional Jewish literature, which extols the Patriarchs. Ethics of the Fathers (5:19) characterizes a disciple of Abraham as possessing "a good eye, a meek spirit, and a humble soul." Evidently, the Mishnah's reading of Genesis leads to the conclusion that Abraham had these superlative attributes. But in fact, this is *not* what we find in Genesis. The Torah's collection of stories and vignettes does not support the idea that the forefathers' behavior was beyond reproach. Indeed, as detailed in appendix 1, out of thirty vignettes from Abraham's life, we discover that roughly one-quarter cast Abraham in a positive light, half cast him in a neutral light, and one-quarter appear to cast him in a negative light. This is hardly a superlative narrative developed to extol Abraham's virtue.

It is surprising to discover this. After all, the forefathers had very long lives. There must have been numerous stories of good deeds and good works that would explain why they were chosen. Why did the Torah not select the stories that align with these objectives? Why is there a mismatch between the picture painted in Ethics of the Fathers and the actual text of the Torah?

The dissonance between Abraham's selection and his worthiness begins with the very introduction of the Patriarch. In 12:2, God promises Abraham that he will become a great nation. But the promise is quite sudden. By what merit? We haven't yet heard one story about Abraham's greatness!

Our Sages were sensitive to this question. Accordingly, the Midrash testifies to Abraham's greatness even prior to chapter 12. For example, the most
noted Torah commentator, Rashi (11:28), cites a Midrash that Abraham was
a noted warrior against idolatry even when he lived in Charan. Apparently,
that was one reason he merited the blessing of greatness in 12:2. But these
events are omitted from the text of the Torah. Why?

Similarly, we do not find a lifelong description of Abraham's acts of loving-kindness. True, there are some isolated examples, such as when Abraham
acts as a good host to the angels in chapter 18 or resolves not to take any
riches from the battlefield (14:23). But these vignettes are rare.

This mismatch is exacerbated by the popular notion that Abraham's outstanding virtue was his *chesed* (loving-kindness). Rashi (18:1) explains that
when the three angels appeared to Abraham, he was sitting by the opening of
his tent looking for wayfarers whom he could help. This produces the popular
image that Abraham's entire being was wrapped up in loving-kindness. This
is reinforced by the Amidah, recited thrice daily by Jews, in which we say that
God "remembers the loving-kindness of the Patriarchs."

Moreover, one of the famous verses of the Prophets is Micah 7:20, in
which the prophet declares, "You will show faithfulness to Jacob, mercy [i.e.,
loving-kindness] to Abraham." Taken literally, the verse means that God
will show mercy to Abraham. But Rashi inverts its meaning, explaining the
verse to mean that God will give rewards in return for Abraham's acts of
loving-kindness toward God. In light of the rabbinic association between
Abraham and *chesed*, we would thus expect that Genesis would be replete
with anecdotes of kindness.

But when we open the text of Genesis, we see that the open tent is just
one of the many vignettes. We can infer loving-kindness from that text, but
most of the vignettes are unrelated to this expected virtue. Why is the Torah
telling us the challenges of Abraham's difficult life rather than focusing on his
qualifications?

Our Sages understood that they needed to probe the purpose of the biblical text. The Mishnah (Ethics of the Fathers 5:3) discusses ten tests that
Abraham needed to pass – one being the requirement to leave his homeland
to go to Canaan. But the text of Genesis does not make clear what was the

substance of the tests, why they were required, or what they proved. We are left with the question of why the heroics are not recorded.

Our approach to these questions is to advance the idea that there was a kernel of merit found in our forefathers that qualified them to be the progenitors of God's Chosen People. Further, identifying these qualifications informs us about the mission of the Chosen People. We will explain the mission of the Chosen People and how it is developed in the biblical narrative. In turn, this will answer the meta-question that we started with: What is the purpose of this text in detail? *Genesis is a roadmap to describe the expected journey of the Chosen People.*

We already mentioned the ten tests of Abraham that our Sages identified. The discussion of Abraham's qualifications will enrich our understanding of the ten tests. We will explain in fine detail how these tests were designed to determine whether Abraham was qualified to be the progenitor of the Chosen People. This will also help us understand when in his life he was chosen. Was he chosen at the outset – at 12:1 – before passing any tests? Was he not chosen until after the ten tests? Did Isaac and Jacob need to be tested?

Superficially, the stories in Genesis appear to be random. We will show, however, that every story is exquisitely selected to characterize the Chosen People. When one reads the biblical text, one gets the impression that there are large numbers of individual stories. Some indeed appear to be fundamental to the principal theme of the Torah – certainly, the births of the forefathers fit into that category. Others seem incidental. We will identify a precise pattern to this narrative related to this theme of qualifications.

Our analysis reveals that chapters 12 to 28 are a single story. They are the story of the qualifications of the Patriarchs and Matriarchs to spawn the Chosen People – nothing more and nothing less. The unified theory of chapters 12–28 needs to be taught as a single narrative with individual vignettes being puzzle pieces to reveal the entire story.

Unique Merit for Abraham and Sarah

Let's take the challenge of identifying Abraham's superlative qualifications one step further.

The apparent flow of Genesis chapter 12 is that God finds a great and worthy person, Abraham, and in recognition of his worthiness, God promises to make Abraham into a great nation. Verse 12:2 is explicit: "I will make of you a great nation, and I will bless you, and make your name great; and you shall be a blessing." The promise is explicit, but Abraham's greatness and worthiness are not.

What do we know about Abraham at this point? He is born (11:26–27), marries Sarah (11:29), who is barren (11:30), and leaves to the land of Canaan with his father Terah and other family members – getting only as far as Charan (11:31). This is hardly the resume of someone who is worthy of the promises of verse 12:2!

To be sure, Abraham is destined to perform good deeds, as we see in the subsequent chapters of Genesis. (It is also true that he will do deeds that appear to be neutral or questionable. See chapter 5 and appendix 1.) But this reinforces the question: With what merit did Abraham deserve these blessings at the beginning of chapter 12? And what was the catalyst that led God to select Abraham as the forefather of the Chosen People?

The Sages understood this issue and developed perspectives about Abraham's achievements that caused him to be selected. For example, they say that he was a champion of monotheism. But that is not an adequate unique explanation of his worthiness. He was not alone in acknowledging God as Creator. Others (e.g., Noah, Shem) recognized God's supremacy (Noah in 6:9; Shem, see below). And the text is not explicit that Abraham's monotheism was the reason for his selection. Furthermore, all the verses that testify to his monotheism occur after God chooses him in 12:2.

Looking before 12:1, the Midrash identifies Abraham as one who unflinchingly allowed himself to be thrown into a burning furnace rather than sacrifice his monotheistic ideals (Rashi 11:28). But if that vignette is key to the biblical storyline, why is it missing from the text? We see many vignettes about Abraham's life explicit in the text. Why omit the foundational heroic story? Doesn't the Torah want us to appreciate the reason for Abraham's selection?

Similarly, Rashi (12:5) asserts that Abraham and Sarah converted people to God's ways back in Charan. This is certainly very praiseworthy, but if that is their key merit, why is it absent from the text?

This lack of approbation is striking when compared to other Torah greats. While Noah's introduction does not include lists of his good deeds, the Torah at least testifies to his goodness. In 6:8, the Torah states, "But Noah found grace in the eyes of the Lord." Verse 6:9 continues with "Noah was in his generations a man righteous and whole-hearted; Noah walked with God." Only after this context is established does God approach Noah in 6:13–18 and share His plan that the world will be destroyed and Noah will be saved. But when the Torah presents Abraham, there is not even an assertion that he was righteous and God-fearing.

Moses' introduction is even more striking. At his birth, we heard that "he was a goodly child" (Exodus 2:2). Before he received any mission from God, he saw the suffering of his people and smote the Egyptian oppressor (Exodus 2:10–12). As a freedom fighter, he needed to flee (Exodus 2:15), and as a stranger in a foreign land saved and helped the hapless daughters of the priest of Midian (Exodus 2:17). Only then do we see God approach Moses in Exodus chapter 3 and identify Moses as the instrument of redemption. But for Abraham, there are no similar precursor heroic deeds or characterization as "good."

The major medieval commentator Ramban (Nachmanides) is sensitive to this question and asks similarly (12:2), why did God tell Abraham to get his reward of the land of Canaan before saying that Abraham was a good and perfect man? He answers that Abraham deserved this reward because the people of Ur made Abraham suffer. But while Ramban clearly understood the question, his answer does not really address it, because, again, the stories of Abraham's travails in Ur are not recorded.

We are left with only Midrashic sources for Abraham's goodness. But if we rely on Midrashic sources, it is still unclear why Abraham was chosen as forefather over other righteous individuals who might have been candidates as well.

We are introduced in 14:18 to a character whose name is Malkizedek. According to Rashi, quoting the Midrash, this character is none other than Shem the son of Noah. He was the king of Salem, which according to the Ramban (and others) was the city of Jerusalem. He is called "a priest to the Most High God," which according to Ramban means that he was a priest to the true God – not to false gods. For that reason, Abraham was agreeable to tithe his earnings to Malkizedek (14:20).

Based on the Midrash, if God wanted to start a branch called the Chosen People, why not start with an earlier heroic individual, Shem? Shem was already a leader – a notable king over the holy city of Jerusalem and a priest as well. One might try to answer this question by pointing out that Shem should not be selected as the Patriarch because he had evil descendants, but this is not dispositive, for Abraham had Esau as an evil descendant as well. In what way, therefore, was Shem less deserving than Abraham?

Shem, like Abraham, had worthy descendants – notably Ever (Shem's great-grandson). Ever, according to the Midrash (see Rashi 28:9), was the teacher of Jacob many years later. Ever could have been chosen as a Patriarch. Both Shem and Ever were still alive when Abraham was selected by God. The selection of Abraham as the unique person "chosen by God" seems not well motivated by the text or Midrash. All of this requires us to understand more about the selection process.

Intermixed into this discussion, then, are three distinct questions:

• What was the unique merit of Abraham and Sarah?
• Was there something about the timing of Abraham's selection that was impactful?
• Was Abraham chosen in 12:2, or was there some longer process?

To address these three questions, chapter 1 will identify the unique character-istics of Abraham and Sarah that qualified them for their roles, based on the text of Genesis. In chapter 3, we will discuss why God chose this moment in history to begin the Chosen People and when exactly Abraham was chosen.

Who Is Included in the Chosen People?

The Chosen People comprises Abraham, Isaac, Jacob, and Jacob's descen-dants. (Also included are converts who choose to be Jewish and their descen-dants.) Apparently, all of Jacob's children are included, but his twin brother Esau and his descendants are excluded. Abraham has several other children – notably Ishmael – who are excluded. The Torah provides several vignettes to explain who is included and what the reasons are.

The criteria to exclude Abraham's descendants (e.g., Esau and Ishmael) are not clear. They might have sinned, but descendants of Jacob who are sinners are included in the Chosen People. We must understand: Is there a clear rationale by which Esau and Ishmael are excluded, but sinning descendants of Jacob are included?

This question is especially sharp when one considers the extent of the sins of Jacob's sons. There are narratives provided in both Genesis and the Midrash that detail these sins. Some are open to interpretation – were they really as bad as they seem to be? The Midrash, for example, provides some justifications for when Shimon and Levi kill an entire city (Genesis chapter 34). But some are unequivocally bad.

For example, Joseph's brothers kidnapped him and sold him into slavery (Genesis chapter 37), after initially plotting to murder him. Clearly that is bad. Any theft is prohibited – this is one of the seven Noahide laws that form the basis of God's instructions for all of humanity (see my book *Genesis: A Torah for All Nations* for more on this). Hence almost all of Jacob's sons were guilty of a capital crime. Yet they all are part of the covenant.

The confusing process of selecting the Chosen People does not stop at Abraham and Sarah. Apparently, Isaac's selection by God is decided even before his birth (see Genesis 17:21). We will explain Isaac's life and focus on two contradictory elements. On the one hand, is Isaac automatically a Patriarch at birth? There is no tradition that he needs to undergo ten tests. Did he need to demonstrate worthiness on his own? It seems that his status is automatic. On the other hand is the dilemma of Esau. If the Chosen People are automatically selected to be the descendants of Abraham and Sarah through their only son Isaac, how is it possible that Jacob's twin, born to the same Isaac and Rebecca, is not included in the Chosen People? That leads us to important further conclusions about how the Patriarchs were qualified for their roles, as well as about Isaac's personality, initiatives, and unique role among the Patriarchs. It also sheds light on the interplay between Jacob and Esau in the house of Isaac and Rebecca, explaining the bizarre spectacle of Isaac apparently wanting to provide preferred blessings to his unworthy son Esau.

A Broader Context

This book is a sequel to *Genesis: A Torah for All Nations*, which covered chapters 1–11 of Genesis. It is a sequel in concept in that it covers the next portion of the Torah, but it is to be read separately.

That book began by summarizing Judaism's approach to different parts of the Torah. As recalled by Rashi (1:1), the primary purpose of the Torah – a book of commandments – comes into focus in Exodus chapter 12 with the first mitzvah incumbent upon the Jewish people. But that results in a huge question: What is the purpose of the prologue that comprises all of Genesis and the first eleven chapters of Exodus?

We looked at the famous answer of Rabbi Yitzchok, quoted in Rashi. The prologue is to demonstrate God's authority over the world and in an elaborate fashion to show God's ability to choose one nation to be close to, to whom He would grant the Holy Land of Israel.

While Rabbi Yitzchok's response explained the macro motivation of this long prologue, it did not come close to explaining the purpose of each and every verse. There are over a thousand verses containing hundreds of stories in Genesis that were included in the Torah for a reason. The analysis of that question resulted in the previous book, which provided a detailed explication of the first eleven chapters of Genesis. We presented a theory that these chapters comprise "a Torah for all nations." Just as the Torah has the purpose of describing the 613 mitzvot that are incumbent on the Jewish people – and the Torah surrounds that description with a rich narrative of vignettes to bring these commandments to life – so too the first eleven chapters of Genesis serve the same purpose for Noahide laws. Judaism believes that there are seven universal Noahide laws that are incumbent on all of mankind. These laws are presented within the first eleven chapters of Genesis and are brought to life in a context of vignettes.

We stopped after these eleven chapters because that was the natural stopping point. Chapter 12 of Genesis begins the stories that establish the Patriarchs and Matriarchs as the founders of the Jewish people who are destined to inherit the Land of Israel. The theme of the remainder of Genesis is different from that of the first eleven chapters.

That leaves the remainder of Genesis to be explored. Rabbi Yitzchok already taught us the high-level purpose of the remainder of Genesis. As Rashi (1:1) quotes: "The strength of His hands He related to His people to give them the inheritance of the nations" (Psalms 111:6). Rashi continues to explain that the purpose of Genesis is to record God's promise that He will select a chosen nation and deed the Land of Israel to them.

As we start analyzing Genesis from the beginning of chapter 12, we see that these chapters are the heart of this promise. Indeed, the promise begins immediately in chapter 12. In Genesis 12:7, God states, "To your seed will I give this land." And throughout the discussion with Abraham, God repeats this promise in various ways several times.

But that does not explain the entire text of Genesis. Apparently, the Torah could have stopped after 12:7. What was the necessity for the remaining thirty-eight chapters of Genesis and the first eleven chapters of Exodus? There must have been some larger purpose.

We note that Jewish literature is full of commentary about Genesis. There is no shortage of morals and lessons that our Sages have taught us about every single verse in Genesis. But the approach that we take is somewhat different.

Our approach is to take a holistic view of Genesis. We start by asking the broad question: What is the overall purpose of having these chapters at all? There must be a significant rationale to the overall flow of Genesis. The Torah did not tell us a collection of vignettes merely for us to infer lessons in minutiae based on the particular word choices of the text. The overarching meaning of chapters 12–28 of Genesis is the investigation that we undertake in this book.

Chapter 1

A Worthy Progenitor

This chapter addresses the fundamental question of this book – finding the source for Abraham's qualification. We are looking for superlative characteristics with the following properties:

- They are text based; i.e., the Torah tells us that Abraham has these characteristics.
- They are logical; i.e., there is a good match between the characteristics and the mission of the Chosen People.
- They are unique; i.e., no other biblical greats (e.g., Shem, Ever) have that collection of characteristics.
- They match up well with what God verifies in the ten tests of Abraham (see chapter 2 of this book).

In addition, we must answer whether and why Abraham was chosen before passing any of the tests.

Often, commentators explain that Abraham's key characteristic is simple faith. After all, in Genesis chapter 12, on God's say-so, Abraham entirely uproots his life to move to Canaan. That is our introduction to Abraham in the biblical story – his first act of qualification.

But it is hard to conclude that this is his only qualifier. Indeed, consider our question above: Why was Abraham chosen instead of Shem or Ever? The qualifications must be unique to Abraham and not apply to Shem and Ever. But presumably, they too had complete faith in God.

Abraham's act of uprooting and transplanting his life to Canaan followed a direct commandment from God. In such circumstances, even lesser people might have complied – it is hard not to comply with a direct suggestion from the Deity.

Blind faith could also not be the solitary qualifier, because we find that Abraham did question God's decisions. He challenged God's decision to destroy Sodom by saying, "Will You indeed sweep away the righteous with the wicked?" (18:25). If we are to find Abraham's qualifications in the biblical text, we need something more specific and more clearly spelled out – an enduring concept that fits Abraham precisely and describes no one else.

The Three Critical Attributes

To determine Abraham's qualifications is difficult. We do not see a job description in Genesis. At the moment of Abraham's initial selection (chapter 12), there is no crisp reason given for the selection. In the absence of the Torah mapping out a specific reason, any proposal would be simple conjecture.

Our approach to answering this question is to look at the text of Genesis that discusses Abraham – chapters 12–25. We find places in the text where the Torah provides superlative descriptions of Abraham. Indeed, there are three instances in which the Torah extols Abraham's personal qualifications:

1. **Belief in God's ethical compass.** The Torah reports, "And he [i.e., Abraham] believed in the Lord, and He counted it to him for righteousness" (15:6).
2. **Ability to transmit the heritage of God's word.** God says about Abraham, "For I have known him, that he may command his children and his household after him, that they may keep the way of the Lord, to do righteousness and justice; to the end that the Lord may bring upon Abraham that which He hath spoken of him" (18:19).
3. **Obedience to God's commands.** An angel of God concludes after the binding of Isaac that various blessings come to Abraham "because you have hearkened to My voice" (22:18).

These characteristics appear to uniquely qualify Abraham. They are explicit in the Torah as his personal characteristics. As we will discuss, these are logical characteristics for the mission of the Chosen People and are not seen in any other great biblical personage. We will also provide the linkage to the ten tests.

The last of Abraham's three qualifying characteristics is repeated several chapters later when God Himself tells Isaac the reason for the promises made to Abraham: "Because that Abraham hearkened to My voice, and kept My charge, My commandments, My statutes, and My laws" (26:5). Rabbi Samson Raphael Hirsch explains (22:18) that the blessings come to Abraham due to his demonstration of obedience. We hear a second time now that the reason for Abraham's selection is his obedience, with an elaboration that this specifically means his fealty to a charge, commandments, statutes, and laws.

The strong statements about obedience in 22:18 and 26:5 are quite direct in associating Abraham's blessings with the characteristic of obedience. Indeed, even the statement about transmission refers to obedience, saying, "that they may keep the way of the Lord" (18:19). One might infer that obedience is the *sole* qualification. But in chapter 2, we will look at how God tested Abraham. Some of the tests (e.g., the battle of the kings) have nothing to do with obedience. So the other two qualifiers must be relevant as well.

The statement about transmission is also clearly a qualification. The last phrase in that statement is "to the end that the Lord may bring upon Abraham that which He hath spoken of him." Rashi explains that phrase as follows. Since Abraham commands his sons to keep the way of the Lord, therefore God can bring upon Abraham what has been promised to him. In other words, commitment to transmission is a qualification to get God's promises and blessings.

Since these three characteristics are called out by the Torah, it is the thesis of this book that these are the qualifications required to be the progenitor of the Chosen People. That will be the basis to explain chapters 12–28 of Genesis. It will explain why this entire text and the specific vignettes are included in the Torah.

Challenging my thesis that *these* three characteristics are the qualifiers is the fact that these three qualities are not Abraham's only positive qualities. Ethics of the Fathers (5:19) credits Abraham as having a good eye, a humble spirit, and a lowly soul. Kehati explains he had a good eye, in part because he gave spoils of war to the king of Sodom and did not take for himself (14:23). Abraham had a humble spirit, as he said that he was dust and ashes (18:27). Abraham had a lowly soul, because when he remarked to Sarah that she was beautiful, it was the first time he had looked at her (12:11). And as we said in the introduction, Abraham was also known for his attribute of loving-kindness.

Although Abraham had these four additional attributes, the text of Genesis does not directly call them out. Hence it is hard to conclude that these four traits are what qualify him for his role as progenitor of the Chosen People. For each of these four attributes, the Sages infer the attributes by looking at vignettes in Abraham's life. But belief in God's ethical compass, commitment to transmission of the heritage of God's words, and obedience to God's commands are unique because:

- It is only in the three verses cited above that the Torah identifies a behavior as a key attribute.
- In all three cases, the Torah itself is extolling the virtue.
- These three are fundamental character traits, not individual actions.
- Specifically, for the quality of obedience, God links the character trait directly to the blessings and hence to Abraham's chosenness (22:18 and 26:5).
- God also singles out Abraham's commitment to transmission of the heritage as deserving of reward.
- We will see in chapter 2 that these are the attributes that are actually tested for in the ten tests.

If these are indeed our three qualifications for the role of founding father of the Chosen People, why does Ethics of the Fathers identify three different characteristics? This is not a difficulty. Certainly Abraham had many positive attributes. In the context of the homiletic messages of Ethics of the Fathers, the Mishnah wanted to emphasize those characteristics that represent a sharp contrast with other biblical notables such as Bilaam (a prophet who attempted to use his abilities to curse the Jews; see Numbers chapters 22–24). But that does not mean that these are the key qualifiers.

It is not sufficient to identify three verses that positively extol Abraham's virtue and assert that these must contain the characteristics required to be chosen. The purpose of this book is to prove this thesis in multiple ways. One proof, as mentioned above, is that these characteristics are explicitly called out. The proofs continue in chapter 2, where we demonstrate that these three attributes are precisely the ones tested for in the ten tests. We continue to use these attributes to clear up other mysteries. One is that although Isaac apparently was automatically included in God's covenant at birth (without undergoing ten tests), his sons were not automatically included; but Jacob's sons were automatically included in the covenant. We are also able to use this understanding to explain Isaac's peculiar attachment to his unworthy son Esau.

We also see these three themes (which we henceforth simplify to the terms "belief," "commitment to transmission," and "obedience") as essential parts of how the Jewish people deserved redemption from Egypt when the time came. When Moses told the slaves that the redemption was at hand, they immediately believed (Exodus 4:31). When it came time to leave Egypt on the eve of redemption, God commanded the slaves to slaughter the Paschal Lamb – the God of Egypt (Exodus 12:21). This is a very hard task to ask of slaves. But they obeyed. And commitment to transmission is fundamental to many aspects of Torah, but specifically regarding the redemption, which is specifically to be communicated and transmitted to children as an intrinsic part of the Passover celebration (Exodus 12:26–27).

Beyond the redemption, these three themes are also constant in Judaism. The first of the Ten Commandments is to recognize that God took us out of Egypt (Exodus 20:2). That is a statement of a basic belief in God. Beyond that, it speaks to a moral purpose: infinite God rescues slaves and provides mitzvot so they can be a holy nation. Obedience, of course, is what the mitzvot are all about. Transmission's centrality can be seen, for example, in the first chapter of Ethics of the Fathers, which traces how the Torah was transmitted from Moses down to leaders since time immemorial. The Torah itself describes a public ceremony in which the Torah is read so that "their children…may hear, and they may learn" (Deuteronomy 31:13).

Even more compelling is that these three attributes help explain the entire narrative of Abraham's life. As mentioned above and detailed in appendix 1, Abraham's life is described by a series of approximately thirty vignettes. What is the structure of these events, and in what way do they encapsulate Abraham's life? We shall demonstrate that looking at Genesis through the prism of these attributes actually reveals a unified story being told not only about Abraham himself, but about the qualifications of the Chosen People.

Elaboration of the Three Critical Attributes

We know what the words *obedience, belief,* and *transmission* mean in a general sense. As qualifiers for the Chosen People, they have a specific meaning. In this section, we will elaborate on the meaning of each of these terms and explain why these three characteristics are critical for the Chosen People.

Obedience

The definition of obedience is straightforward – one must obey God's laws. But let's put into context why that is a critical characteristic for the Chosen People.

The centrality of "obedience" makes perfect sense in the context of the Torah. Recall the dictum of Rabbi Yitzchok, cited above in the introduction. The entire purpose of the Torah is to provide commandments that are to be obeyed. The commandments begin in Exodus, and Genesis is a prologue. The prologue sets the qualifications for the Chosen People who will get the Torah. First and foremost, they must listen to and obey the commandments.

On the one hand, this statement is so obvious that it seems banal. Of course we are to listen to the commandments. But the reality is that it is not so simple. Man's inclination is to do evil (6:5 and 8:21). Adam and Eve in the Garden of Eden could not observe one law; they could not resist temptation (3:6). The generation of the deluge could not fulfill the seven Noahide laws (6:12). As God prepares to extend the seven laws to the 613 mitzvot incumbent upon Jews, the standard bearer must meet high expectations.

Obedience as a fundamental pillar finds a voice when the chosenness of the Jews is confirmed at Sinai. What do the Jewish people do to demonstrate that they are worthy to receive the Torah at Sinai? In Exodus 24:7, the Jews cry out, *Na'aseh v'nishma* (We will obey and we will hear). They agreed to obey even before they heard what they were accepting. We see the fundamental value of obedience.

Our verse identifies that Abraham kept "My charge, My commandments, My statutes, and My laws" (26:5). This verse is discussed in the Mishnah (*Kiddushin* 4:14). The Mishnah is trying to understand the rationale for the itemization of "charge," "commandments," "statutes," and "laws." Does this itemization imply that the verse includes more than the seven Noahide laws? The Sages' response is that Abraham observed the entire Torah (i.e., 613 mitzvot) even before it was given. Indeed, an extraordinary commitment to obedience.

Belief

Superficially, it is hard to explain why Abraham's simple belief in God was extraordinary. Abraham had a personal relationship with God. God spoke to him. God gave him commands such as "move to Canaan." It is not hard to believe in a Deity Who is speaking to you.

But our definition of belief is much deeper. To see that, let's look at the proof text of 15:6. In 15:5, God had promised Abraham that he would have descendants. When 15:6 reports that Abraham believed, this does not refer to a belief in God. God is right in front of him. It can't only mean that he believed that God existed.

When the Torah talks about Abraham's belief, it means that *Abraham believed in an involved, ethical God Who cares about what happens on earth.* In other words, he believed without a doubt that a commitment made by God will be fulfilled. God is a personal God involved in the destiny of mankind. That is His ethical compass. That type of belief is special. Both Sforno and Ramban emphasize that it was this belief – that God would fulfill the commitments without any doubt – that comprised the meaning of the word *belief* in 15:6.

Although there was no reason for God *not* to fulfill His promise, it was still a revolutionary act of faith on Abraham's part to trust that God would fulfill His promise. Why should mortal man believe that infinite, inscrutable God cares enough about what happens on Earth? No other person of that day would believe that would happen. But without even asking for a sign, Abraham believed.

Belief does not mean blind faith. God doesn't actually demand or expect blind faith. It was appropriate of Abraham to question God about Sodom (18:23–33). Even in Genesis chapter 15, with the promise of offspring to the childless Abraham, God did not expect blind faith. In 15:7, God continues to promise the Land of Israel as an inheritance. But in 15:8, Abraham asks for a proof for that inheritance. What happened to Abraham's belief? As pointed out by Rashi on 15:6, why does he ask for a proof for the inheritance (15:8) and not for the descendants (15:6)? Is his asking for a proof for the inheritance an indication of lack of belief?

The Ramban on 15:6 compounds this question. Ramban asks: Given that Abraham kept his faith through many trials and tribulations of life, why is it considered so noteworthy that he would keep the faith when he is given such a *positive* promise about descendants? Why is Abraham extolled for belief at that exact place in the text? He should be credited for believing throughout the harder tribulations. That's what requires greater faith!

The commentator *Devek Tov* explains this contrast within Rashi and thereby why it made sense to ask for a sign for the promise about the Land of Israel. Abraham understood that there were prior residents of Canaan. How could God promise to dispossess these inhabitants? Maybe these people would repent their evil ways and not deserve to be removed. Abraham had good reason to suspect that the commitment was not ironclad. Abraham was worried that to fulfill this commitment, God might need to do the impossible – suspend the rules of reward and punishment – and hence not fulfill the commitment. After all, God must care for the planet in a way that does not contradict His ideals. For that reason, in verse 15:8, Abraham took the extraordinary step of asking for a sign. And it was noncontroversial for Abraham to ask for a sign that God would make such an extraordinary commitment. In some sense, Abraham's questioning was an expression of belief. The sign was required to assure that the land grant would be consistent with God's need to operate on an ethical plane.

The commentator Kli Yakar takes a similar approach. He first deepens the question. When God *initially* promised Canaan to Abraham (12:7), why didn't Abraham ask for a sign at that point? He explains that in 12:7, God was promising a *gift* of the land – and no one could possibly complain about a gift. However, in 15:8, when God promised the land as an *inheritance*, this could cause the current residents of the land to complain.

However, for the commitment of descendants (15:5), Abraham saw no path whereby God wouldn't fulfill the commitment. It didn't depend on the righteousness or wickedness of others. It was totally in God's hands to simply fulfill the wish. Hence no sign was required.

Even though Abraham didn't require a sign from God about descendants, Isaac's birth was still extraordinary. Isaac was born in a near-miraculous fashion to a one-hundred-year-old Abraham and ninety-year-old Sarah. Although they did not require a sign per se, when the extraordinary event took place, Sarah saw the need to express something. After the birth has taken place, Sarah says, "Who would have said to Abraham, that Sarah should suckle children? For I have borne him a son in his old age" (21:7).

A simple interpretation of this verse is that Sarah is expressing wonder at the event. But Rashi interprets her words to be praise to God. Sarah is saying how great God is that He promises and fulfills. Part of the mission of transmission is to publicly highlight this unique belief in an involved, caring God Who makes promises and fulfills them.

That belief is fundamental is seen elsewhere in Judaism. The Rambam (Maimonides) starts *Mishneh Torah* (*Hilchot Yesodei Hatorah* 1:1) by saying that the foundation of all foundations is to know that there is a Primary Being (i.e., God). The first of the Ten Commandments is belief in the God Who took the Jewish people out of Egypt (Exodus 20:2). The first of the Rambam's principles of faith is belief in God.

This more developed concept of belief – that God has an ethical basis for the world and remains involved in it – is central as a qualifier for the Chosen People. From time immemorial, people have believed in powers beyond man who created the universe. But it is a jump from naïve belief in unknown powers to believe that an immensely powerful God cares about one species of life, on one planet, in an unimpressive solar system.

That is the uniqueness of Abraham's belief. Many people believed in God. Only Abraham appreciated the extent to which He cares. And that is critical to the mission of the Chosen People. The purpose of the Chosen People is for them to mentor the world in observing the laws of the God Who cares. Related to this is the book of Nehemiah. There it is said about Abraham, "and foundest his heart faithful before you" (9:7–8). Nehemiah continues to explain that it was Abraham's faithfulness that led to God's covenant with him.

Said differently, without a belief in God's involvement in the world, the previous characteristic of obedience becomes unmotivated. Our requirement to obey is anchored on helping God in His quest for morality in the world. But that only makes sense if God Himself is involved in the world.

We mentioned above that in chapter 2, we will see that Abraham is tested for his belief. He is generally required to believe that God fulfills His commitments. But he is not required to believe that God will always do miracles for him; in fact, that would be contrary to the natural order.

It is interesting, however, to see the same concept of "testing" related to belief used later in the Torah. In Exodus (17:2), as the Jews enter the desert, they complain that there is no water. In fact, they are looking for a miraculous solution to the problem. In 17:7, they ask whether they can assume that God is with them if these miracles do not occur. This is testing turned on its head. Instead of God testing a Patriarch on whether he believes that God is involved in the world, this is the nation testing God by insisting that He be involved in the world to the level of providing miracles.

But belief that God will miraculously meet our every need is not our belief system. In Deuteronomy (6:16), there is a specific injunction not to test God in that way.

Commitment to Transmission

The simple attribute of commitment to transmission – to teach one's children – is a basic expectation of life. All people impart some of their value system to their children. But Abraham's involvement in transmission is far greater.

When Abraham's commitment is first described in 18:19, the emphasis is on the family, on establishing a clan with permanent responsibility to observe the word of God. Hence the emphasis in that verse about Abraham commanding this path to his children. Not only his children but also *beito acharav* (his household after him). This expression conveys not only his personal ministry, but his family's as well. The word *beito* is often interpreted by our Sages to mean one's wife (e.g., Mishnah *Yoma* 1:1).

Beyond that, our Sages saw in the language of the verse that Abraham aspired to spread God's word beyond his family. The thirteenth-century commentator Radak emphasizes the focus on educating the entire staff of Abraham's home. The goal was to establish a global legacy of commitment to God's path. Abraham was an evangelist who spread the word to all who would listen. We already mentioned (Rashi 12:5) that even in Charan, Abraham and

Sarah had made it their lives' work to convert everyone to the proper practice of God's commandments.

Thus, the attribute of commitment to transmission has two components. First was the establishment of a family, a clan, a nation for whom spreading the word of God was a national obsession. This was the quality that *most* qualified Abraham for the role of being the progenitor of the Chosen People, because he was acting out the mission that was to be the cohesive glue for the Chosen People. Secondly, there was the component of spreading the word of God universally.

Abraham's obsession to establish a clan that would spread the word of God is evident in 15:2, where Abraham tells God about his frustrations. There is nothing that God can give him, seeing as he is going childless. Ramban and others explain that despite the fact that God had already promised that Abraham would have children (12:7), Abraham was concerned that he might not deserve fulfillment of the promise, because perhaps he had sinned along the way.

The fact that Abraham felt compelled to create a *family* of those who observe God's commandments emphasizes the role of Sarah. Their relationship was more than matrimony. They had a common mission of transmission. That required a family. The idea of transmission was a joint idea. For example, in 12:5, as mentioned above, Rashi explains that they were a duo of proselytizers back in Charan. In Genesis chapter 18, when three angels arrived uninvited, both Abraham and Sarah played a role in welcoming them. And the message of 18:19 was that this family commitment would grow to being a national commitment. Sarah was his wife. Insofar as Hagar was his concubine, the family mission could not be achieved through her.

This does not contradict the great love that Abraham had for Ishmael, nor the notion that Abraham wanted Ishmael to similarly follow the family's mission of belief, observance, and transmission. In terms of bringing people close to God, Abraham was a universalist. He wanted everyone to be on the right path, and certainly his own son Ishmael. But the core goal was to establish a family and a nation of role models. And that nation started with his wife.

There is another indication that the mission of transmission is more than passing one's values to one's children. The verse says, "his children and his household after him." The final qualifier "after him" seems superfluous. Of course his children are after him! This expression emphasizes something beyond basic transmission to one's own children. It projects a later time – after him – a permanent commitment of all descendants.

Sforno makes a related point. In 17:7, God says that the covenant with Abraham extends to his descendants forever. In 18:19 (s.v. "*v'shamru*"), Sforno links 18:19 to 17:7. Sforno is saying that the key to God setting up an eternal covenant with Abraham is exactly Abraham's commitment of setting up an eternal transmission of God's pathways to his clan.

The qualification of commitment to transmission is crucial to the mission of the Chosen People because it is what extends beyond Abraham as an individual and enables God to make a covenant with an entire people – the Chosen People. This is unique. Without transmission, there is no Chosen People for Abraham to be the progenitor of! God's laws apply both to individuals and to communities. To have a covenant with a "people" requires a *mesorah* – a transmission.

To see how Abraham was superlative in transmission, recall that he strove to transmit the mission of godliness to the *entire* world. Abraham's attitude was not limited to transmitting in a cultic way only to his descendants. There were many great personalities throughout the history of the world: Adam, Noah, Shem, Ever. But none had Abraham's intensity of fervor to spread the message. While universal transmission was not a minimum requirement for this job, we do see how much Abraham excelled.

Indeed, the Talmud (*Avodah Zarah* 9a) talks about a "two-thousand-year" time period for the teaching of the Torah. The Sages ask: What is the beginning of the period of the Torah? They conclude that the period of the story started when Abraham and Sarah started teaching Torah to non-Jews in Charan. This teaches us two things. First, it is a reaffirmation that one of the key qualifiers for the progenitor of the Chosen People was his activity in transmitting the Torah. Second, we see that he was so qualified – he was a universal transmitter to all who would listen.

This desire to transmit the word of God widely is seen in Abraham's name. In 17:5, God changes his name from Abram to Abraham. The rationale is that the latter name means that Abraham is the "father of a multitude of nations." This could be understood in the physical sense – that Abraham was the progenitor of the Jewish nation as well as the nations that emanated from

Ishmael and Esau, etc. But that physical sense is devoid of moral importance. Those were not "chosen" nations. What is the relevance? An explanation that is in line with Abraham's ministry is that he is the father of both the Jewish nation and any person who is willing to accept the transmitted word of the true God. To this day, when a name is given to a convert to Judaism, Abraham is designated as the father of the convert.

What is it that Abraham is transmitting? In the broadest sense, he is transmitting the word of God. He is transmitting to his descendants and to the world that people must live a godly path.

But in keeping with our analysis that there are three key qualifications – obedience, belief, and commitment to transmission – it is apparent that the other two qualifications are what Abraham needs to transmit. Thus commitment to transmission wraps up the qualifications into one whole.

Where do we see that transmission includes the transmission of belief? Radak (18:1, s.v. "*va'yera*") explains the purpose of the angelic visits of Genesis chapter 18. The purpose of their coming and of Abraham receiving advance knowledge of the destruction of Sodom was so that Abraham should know that God involves Himself on earth to reward and punish according to people's actions. Radak links this message to the transmission verse of 18:19. God informed Abraham of the destruction of Sodom so that Abraham would have the explicit knowledge to inform his descendants that the destruction was an instantiation of what we must believe. God's involvement in reward and punishment is exactly what belief is about. It is not about simple belief in the existence of God. It is belief that God is involved in this world – assuring its ethical plane through reward and punishment.

That transmission includes the importance of obedience is pointed out by many commentaries on 18:19:

- Rashi explains that the transmission is that the descendants should follow God's path.
- Radak repeats that the transmission is to follow God's path (to be rewarded).
- Rabbenu Chananel emphasizes that the transmission is to follow all of God's commandments – both what is received orally and that which is written in the Torah.

Recall the Rashi on Micah 7:20 we brought above in the introduction. We explained that according to Rashi, God was rewarding Abraham for the latter's loving-kindness. But Rashi takes it a step further by defining what it means that Abraham had the attribute of loving-kindness. It is not only that Abraham is warm, loving, and helpful to his fellow man. Rashi in Micah explains that Abraham expresses loving-kindness *to God*, precisely by taking on the mission of transmission. God needs someone to pick up the baton, and Abraham steps up to the task. Hence there is a linkage between the characteristic of transmission and the attribute of loving-kindness.

The Uniqueness of Abraham

That linkage, then, brings us to the key question: What was unique about Abraham that he would merit being the progenitor of the Chosen People?

We need to compare Abraham to his contemporary notables. We posit that during Abraham's time, God was looking to establish a Chosen People (more about that later). God could have started with anyone, but He chose Abraham, who must have been more suited than other notables.

Specifically, why wasn't the title of chosenness given to the notables Shem and Ever? It seems clear that Shem and Ever fulfilled the qualification of obedience. They are recorded in text and lore as great leaders. Shem was a priest to God (14:18; see also Rashi there). Ever was the teacher of Jacob (Rashi 28:9). It must be that they obeyed God's commandments. And by teaching Jacob, Ever was somewhat involved in transmission as well.

It is unknown how much they demonstrated belief. Certainly, as dedicated teachers and priests – perhaps even prophets (see Rashi 25:23) – they must have believed in God. But did they possess the greater belief in an involved God Who keeps His commitments? We don't know.

There is no record of their transmitting the faith to their children. Shem's most notable son was Arpachshad (11:10), and there is no record of greatness about him. Ever's most notable son was Peleg (11:16), who was mostly known as a contemporary of the Tower of Babel (10:25).

It seems plausible that Shem and Ever did not excel at transmission at the same level as Abraham. As discussed above, transmission is fundamental to being able to create a Chosen People. That could be a clear disqualifier.

Additionally, perhaps even their belief in an involved God did not reach Abraham's level.

These reasons might not be the only reasons that Shem and Ever were not selected. The Talmud was bothered by this question and came up with the following answer. The Talmud (*Nedarim* 32b) explains that when Shem blessed God and Abraham (14:19–20), he erred by blessing Abraham first. Because of this error, he lost the ability to pass the priesthood to his son. We see several things:

- The Talmud was also sensitive to the issue of why Shem was not selected.
- Indeed, Shem was a candidate, but he lost his candidacy due to some action of his.
- It is interesting how the Talmud says it: due to this error, Shem was a priest, but his son was not. We see some linkage between Shem's deselection and the lack of a transmission on his part.

The Characteristics for the Chosen People

Putting this all together, Abraham as an individual exhibits the key personal characteristics that God insists on from everyone – belief and obedience. Those are the basic requirements. This is a high-level belief – appreciating the moral scope of the Torah and God's involvement in the world. To give rise to the Chosen People also requires transmission. Abraham and Sarah are signing up for a ministry. They will spread the word of God. That's their differentiation. All three of these characteristics are noted explicitly by verses in the text.

We have three characteristics: belief, obedience, and commitment to transmission. What evidence was there at the outset that Abraham would excel in these areas? This relates to the question of when the choice of Abraham was finalized.

We now discuss why the beginning of the choice of Abraham occurred in 12:1, before the first of the ten tests. By openly proselytizing to idolators in Charan (Rashi 12:5), Abraham was demonstrating that he had the right inclinations toward those qualifications. He was demonstrating belief, obedience, and commitment to transmission in difficult circumstances. At some level, he was self-tested, so he was a prime candidate to be chosen.

With that pre-test, Abraham emerged as a candidate. Now God asked him to move to Canaan and face a more rigorous set of tests. This would ensure that in Abraham's case, these characteristics were ironclad. Genesis 12–25, as understood by our Sages, is the narrative of Abraham being tested (Ethics of the Fathers 5:3). When the Sages said that Abraham underwent ten tests, they did not mean that God decided on a random set of exams for Abraham. The tests were the formal qualifiers that tested these three characteristics. Without passing these tests, Abraham could not have been the progenitor of the Jewish people.

Understanding what qualified Abraham is a critical part of understanding the role of the Chosen People. For if belief, obedience, and commitment to transmission are what qualified Abraham to start the Chosen People, then it is axiomatic that the mission of the Chosen People is to exhibit these properties and live their lives with these values.

The requirement of belief is evident. As we mentioned above, so many fundamental Jewish texts (the Rambam's Thirteen Principles of Faith, the Ten Commandments) start with belief. And as we said above, this is not simple belief in God. This is belief in a moral, caring God Who keeps His commitments. That is why the first of the Ten Commandments asked not just that we believe in God, but that we believe in the God Who fulfilled His commitment to take us out of Egypt.

Obedience is also evident. The 613 mitzvot are commanded to the Jewish people so that they be obeyed. This is consistent with Rabbi Yitzchok's theory that the purpose of Genesis is as a broad introduction to the mitzvot that begin to be enumerated in Exodus chapter 12. Here Genesis is setting the stage for a book (the Torah) that is written in order to be obeyed.

Transmission teaches us an important lesson. The mission of the Chosen People is not to be a cloistered group that follows some practice for its own sake. The purpose is to popularize the importance of worshipping the true God.

Chapter 2

Abraham's Ten Tests

A central theme of Genesis 12–25 is Abraham's ten tests. When one examines these ten tests, we see that they are precisely testing for the three characteristics of belief, obedience, and commitment to transmission. That is aligned with our overall theme from many points of view:

- This confirms that these characteristics were the critical ingredients for Abraham to demonstrate, as progenitor of the Chosen People.
- It shows the care that God put into selecting Abraham as the progenitor. He wanted him to be well tested before finalizing the selection.
- Earlier, we were looking for an organizing thread that explains why the Torah chooses to relate these thirty particular vignettes about Abraham's life. The fact that the vignettes contain the tests reveals a logic to their selection.
- This context begins to explain why the behaviors of Abraham were not necessarily positive or heroic (see the introduction and appendix 1). The purpose of the Torah was not to demonstrate heroics. It was to illustrate how the qualifying characteristics were tested.

The Imperative to Test

Given mankind's previous evils, it is not surprising that God wanted a rigorous testing regimen. God had observed about mankind prior to the deluge that "*every* imagination of the thoughts of his heart was *only* evil continually" (6:5; my emphasis). In the immediate aftermath of the deluge, the assessment improved but was still grim: "the imagination of man's heart is evil from his youth" (8:21). Then there was the Tower of Babel (11:1–9) – a rebellion against God.

What was God's methodology? God confronted Abraham with situations that would shatter the belief of a lesser man; Abraham needed to be steadfast.

God assigned seemingly impossible tasks; Abraham needed to obey instructions. God created situations that could prevent Abraham from accomplishing his life's mission of transmission – his raison d'être. Abraham needed to plow forward, undaunted in those situations, and lead his life. Abraham needed to pass the tests to demonstrate his worthiness.

Ethics of the Fathers (5:3) states that there are ten tests. But they are not listed, and based on the Torah and the Midrash, Abraham endured more than ten challenges in his life. Different commentators have different interpretations.

The Rambam, in his explanation of Ethics of the Fathers 5:3, lists ten that are all found in the Torah itself:

1. Departing Charan to move to Canaan (12:1)
2. A famine (12:10)
3. Taking Sarah to Pharoah (12:15)
4. The battle of four kings versus five (chapter 14)
5. Abraham's taking of Hagar (16:3)
6. Circumcision at age ninety-nine (17:10)
7. The king of Gerar taking Sarah (20:2)
8. God's command to send away Hagar (21:12)
9. The expulsion of Ishmael (21:12)
10. The binding of Isaac (chapter 22)

Given we claim that the three attributes of belief, obedience, and commitment to transmission are the qualifications and that the tests are the qualifiers, there must be some mapping between the tests and the attributes. That's how the tests demonstrate that Abraham has the necessary capability.

The first nine tests are arranged in three groups of three. In each of the three groups, there is one test for obedience, one for belief, and one for commitment to transmission. At every step of the way, God is testing Abraham on all characteristics.

The tenth test is the final exam. It is a single exam that simultaneously tests all three characteristics. In the remainder of this chapter, we will discuss the testing for each of the three characteristics.

Certain trials and tribulations of Abraham's life are not counted as tests. God's revelation to Abraham that God intended to destroy Sodom was not one of the tests. Why did the Rambam not include that situation as a test? Apparently, it did not challenge belief, obedience, or commitment to transmission. Rather, it *reinforced* belief in a just God. There was nothing to obey. Sodom was not a primary focus of Abraham's transmission, in any case.

Also, Abraham's reaction to hearing about Sodom's destruction – challenging God's decision – was not a test. He was asking whether there were righteous people on whose account Sodom deserved to be spared (18:23). He was not violating belief. It is true that he challenged God. But it was not a fundamental issue.

The most vexing challenge in Abraham's life was being without children. He did not have a child until he reached age eighty-six and had Ishmael, and Isaac was not born until Abraham was a hundred. So one might ask why the Rambam does not include childlessness as one of his challenges.

At a purely technical level, it is possible that childlessness is not listed because it was not a specific event. It is not a particular challenge that suddenly confronted Abraham. Rather, it was a constant gnawing lack in his life.

There may be a deeper explanation. Several of these tests bring into focus that Sarah had not borne a child to Abraham. Examples are Sarah's being taken by various kings (test 3 and test 7). Abraham's relationship with Hagar (test 5 and test 8). Indeed, childlessness is not listed as a test – but it is implied by those tests that are related.

Testing for Obedience

Obedience is demonstrated when God asks Abraham to perform a very difficult task and Abraham does it without question. Evidently tests 1, 6, and 8 have that attribute. In each of those three cases, God directly asks Abraham to do something that is very difficult: exile from home (test 1), physical pain (test 6), and breaking up of a family (test 8). In all cases, Abraham does what is asked of him without question. We'll come back to the binding of Isaac (test 10), which also has strong elements of obedience.

Test 1, exile from home, is not merely being asked to leave his home. As pointed out by the Ohr Hachayim, Abraham was not initially told where he was going. He was obedient going into the abyss – "to the land that I will show you" (12:1), without even knowing which land he was going to.

Regarding test 6, some are bothered by Rashi (18:1), which seems to imply that Abraham consulted with the local leader Mamre before deciding to go ahead with the circumcision. Others say that Abraham never questioned the circumcision act, but Mamre advised Abraham to be public about it. In any event, it is known that at the age of ninety-nine, Abraham circumcised himself in obedience to God's command to do so.

Modern psychologists have a deep understanding of which life experiences are most stressful. Any move from one house to another is considered a major stress. How much more so when a person must leave his home, his family, and all of his surroundings (test 1). From a physical point of view, any surgical procedure (test 6) is painful. Finally, divorce (test 8) is rated as an item of considerable stress.

Testing for Belief in a Caring God

Let's recall that the attribute of "belief" does not simply mean belief in God. It refers specifically to belief in an involved, ethical God Who fulfills His commitments, demonstrating that He cares about what happens on earth.

Testing for belief requires a situation in which God seems on a path to break a commitment. Such a situation is designed to cause doubt and consternation. If God were to break a commitment, Abraham might ask: Does God care about what happens on earth? Is God just some cold, amoral force? If Abraham believed that even for a moment, it would sow doubt in his worthiness. A test designed to evaluate the level of his belief would determine whether Abraham would interpret the situation correctly or mistakenly conclude that God is not seriously involved in the world.

Tests 2, 4, and 9 fit that description. In 12:1–2, God tells Abraham that He will make him into a great nation when he goes to Canaan. Yet in 12:10, a famine chases Abraham out of the land before he has achieved greatness (test 2). That could have caused doubt about God's commitment. Why would God promise greatness to Abraham in Canaan and for no apparent reason force him to leave Canaan? But Abraham still believed.

Abraham had a close relationship with Lot. After all, not only are we taught that Lot went to Canaan with Abraham (12:4), it was actually repeated in the next verse (12:5) that Abraham took Lot. Lot was an intimate member of the household. Abraham probably felt that the promise of greatness was extended to his nephew. Yet in chapter 14, in the battle of the kings (test 4), Lot was captured. Abraham was so distraught that he launched a strong counteroffensive. There, Lot is called "his brother" (14:14).

This incident could have challenged Abraham's belief. There was potential diminution of Abraham's reputation and consequent damage to the promise that Abraham would be a great nation. If God cared, why would He let that happen? Still, Abraham believed. Abraham never questioned why God created a situation that would seemingly contradict His commitment to make Abraham into a great nation. To make matters worse, Rashi (14:1) identifies one of the capturing kings as Abraham's nemesis, Nimrod.

How do we know that issues around Lot could cause a diminution of Abraham's reputation? The Talmud discusses this point in treating a different vignette in which Lot indirectly diminished Abraham's reputation: the story of Lot and his daughters.

In the days of the Talmud, when the Torah was read to the people, it would also be translated into Aramaic, the vernacular tongue at that time. *Megillah* 25b discusses various passages that are read but not translated. Typically, they might not be translated if they would confuse the common man or if they would cause embarrassment of some sort.

Megillah 25b asserts that the embarrassing story of Lot and his daughters (19:31–38) *should* be translated. The Talmud asks why this must be specified and concludes that otherwise, we would have thought we should not translate the episode due to the dishonor it would cause Abraham. While in the end, we go ahead with the translation, we do see that the embarrassment caused to Abraham by Lot is recognized by the Talmud as a real concern.

We also see the strength of Abraham's belief in his reaction to Lot's capture. The odds were stacked against him. These powerful four kings who captured Lot had also won a battle with five other kings. The text itself builds up the extent to which Abraham believed. The enemies must have been immensely strong. Nimrod was identified as a mighty hunter (10:9). Abraham had no army, no battle experience, and no soldiers. Yet he went into battle unhindered. He had faith that the God Who had made promises to him was involved in the world and would assure his victory.

Radak (14:1) explains the test more simply. He explains that for Abraham – an individual with a modest group of followers – to take on the four dominating kings in battle was inherently an example of unrestrained faith in God's involvement. How else to explain why he would take this on when he was so outnumbered? It wasn't simple belief in God or even the specific belief that God fulfills commitments, but belief that God would save him against all odds.

That brings us to test 9, the expulsion of Ishmael. As best as we can tell from the text of the Torah and from Midrashim, Abraham always assumed that Ishmael could be redeemed. In 16:15, Abraham names him with a name of God – Ishmael – presumably because God heard the distress of Hagar (16:11). This was a nobler name than that of the Patriarch Isaac, whose Hebrew name, Yitzchak, refers to laughter over a child being born to elderly parents. Also, the Torah emphasizes in 16:15 that Hagar birthed a son *to Abraham* – Abraham fully considered Ishmael to be his son.

Let's look further into the relationship between Abraham and Ishmael to appreciate better the impact of the expulsion of Ishmael.

In 17:18, God tells Abraham that he will have a son with Sarah. Remarkably, Abraham does not thank God. Instead, in 17:20, he beseeches God that Ishmael should live a godly life. Abraham would have been satisfied for Ishmael to be the designated heir; perhaps he would prefer it. He doesn't require a second son. God responds that Isaac is the designated heir, but Abraham should not worry – Ishmael too will be great. Abraham does not answer this. He is not mollified by Ishmael's secondary role, even if Ishmael will also be great. Abraham does not yet accept that anything would be wrong with Ishmael also being a designated heir.

Actually, he goes the other way. In the next chapter, when the angels come to repeat the message to Abraham and Sarah, we see that Abraham prepares a feast for them. He involves his son Ishmael to teach him the mitzvah of loving-kindness – by having guests (see Rashi 18:7, s.v. "*el hana'ar*"). He is doubling down on his efforts to include Ishmael in the covenant.

At the binding of Isaac, God commands Abraham to take "your son, your only son, whom you love, even Isaac" (22:2). Rashi famously explains the progression. When instructed to take his son, Abraham exclaims, "My son? I have two sons." God replies, "Your only son," to which Abraham rejoinders,

"My only son? Each is an only son to his mother." God further specifies, "The son whom you love." Abraham retorts, "Whom I love? I love them both." At that point, God has to come right out and identify Isaac. When Isaac was thirty-seven years old and Ishmael was fifty-one, as the Sages clarify their respective ages at the time of the binding of Isaac, Abraham still did not accept that there was any difference between them. (We know Isaac was thirty-seven because Rashi tells us [23:2, s.v. *"lispod"*] that Sarah died as a result of the binding; she was 90 at his birth and 127 at her death.)

And according to the Sages, Abraham was not wrong to have faith in Ishmael. Rashi (25:9) states that Ishmael repented for his sins. In the end, he was worthy as well.

Abraham had every reason to believe that Ishmael would be part of the Chosen People. After all, Abraham's raison d'être was to teach *everyone* about God. Certainly, his own son was included. In 12:2, God promised to make Abraham into a great nation. There was no restrictive clause stating that only some of his descendants would be part of that great nation. For the first fourteen years of Ishmael's life, he was Abraham's only son. There must have been a strong bond.

After Abraham's death, God blesses Isaac (25:11). Rashi points out that Abraham never blessed Isaac. Rashi explains that Abraham was reluctant to do so, knowing that Esau would come from Isaac. This is a strange reaction. Given that Abraham knew that Isaac is the successor, why can't he bless Isaac? After all, he provided physical possessions to Isaac (25:5).

Aligned with our general observations about the relationship between Abraham and Ishmael, we can offer a modified reason to address Rashi's question. Perhaps Abraham had still not gotten over his regret that Ishmael was not included in the covenant? Perhaps that held Abraham back from providing a formal blessing to Isaac, which might have been seen as a snub to Ishmael.

Back to test 9. Abraham had the unshakable belief that God keeps His commitments. In 15:6, Abraham was so certain about God's commitment to Abraham's descendants that he did not even ask for a sign. Imagine Abraham's distress when Sarah told him, "Cast out this bondwoman and her son" (21:10). Even worse, she continued, "for the son of this bondswoman shall not be heir with my son" (ibid.). Abraham was not predisposed to accept Sarah's words, disinheriting Ishmael. Imagine the crashing pain when God said, "in all that Sarah says to you, listen to her voice" (21:12). That's it. Ishmael is expelled. Ishmael is the son whom Abraham loves. And that seems to contradict God's commitment about descendants that the Torah said Abraham believed (15:6).

This is a test. This tests whether Abraham truly believes in God and His commitments as Abraham understood them. Will Abraham accept God's explanation that it is sufficient for the inheritance to be limited to Isaac (21:12)? What does Abraham do? In 21:14, he does what he is told by God. He wakes up early in the morning, highlighting his rush to implement God's decision. He demonstrates his belief by not questioning God. He does not protest. He accepts that God's commitment will be fulfilled in a different way from what Abraham expected.

Testing for Commitment to Transmission

Abraham had an innate desire to transmit God's word to his descendants and to the world at large. But first, there had to be descendants. Abraham's concept of the mission would be most tested if the connection of that mission through his wife Sarah was tested. That is why tests 3, 5, and 7 were the ones that revealed whether Abraham would be constant about the mission of transmission despite adversity.

In tests 3 and 7, God put Abraham and Sarah in an impossible situation. Abraham had one choice – to be honest – which would result in his certain death. The death might be noble but would destroy his mission. The other choice was to lose Sarah, the lynchpin of the family mission. He was between the proverbial rock and hard place. What was he to do? Would the incident dissuade him from his life's mission of transmission?

Abraham's passing these tests is most evident after test 3. What did Abraham do in the immediate aftermath of almost losing Sarah in Egypt? He went right back to his mission. The Torah relates that he went "to the place where his tent had been at the beginning" (13:3). Again, the Torah says, "to the place of the altar, which he had made there at the first" (13:4). These mild statements must have had a purpose. The purpose was to show Abraham's steadfastness. Despite the shock of the events of Egypt, once Sarah was back in his home, they continued their work. Nothing could stop the mission. He passed the test.

A somewhat different response occurred after the incident in Gerar. The Torah immediately moves to the next vignette – the birth of Isaac (chapter 21). God saw that Abraham continued in his dedication to the mission and now set out to remove the one block preventing it – to bestow onto Abraham a family so he could proceed.

Test 5, the taking of Hagar, similarly tested Abraham's resolve with respect to his mission. At age seventy-five, Abraham moved with Sarah to Canaan. Not having any children, they must have been uplifted by God's message that Abraham would become great in Canaan (12:2). They must have been further uplifted when God promised the land to Abraham's descendants (12:7). Suddenly, Abraham knew there would be descendants.

But ten years later, when Abraham was eighty-five, there were still no children. Despondency set in. What would become of their mission? In desperation, Sarah recommended that Abraham take Hagar. This was not the vision that Abraham and Sarah had of their mission. This was a solid break from his expectation that together with Sarah, they would form a permanent clan of devotion to God. Yet Abraham trusted his mate and did what he was told. And for fifteen long years, from the marriage of Hagar and Abraham until the birth of Isaac, Abraham proceeded with his mission without question. He never wavered from his beliefs and actions, despite the long wait.

Above, we asked why childlessness was not considered a test. Part of our answer is that it was implied in the other tests, such as test 5. These tests demonstrate Abraham's complete faith: he was able to believe that he could complete his life's work – including the mission of transmission – despite many years without a proper heir.

Final Exam

Abraham passed nine tests. It was time for the final exam.

One would think that God should have already been convinced that Abraham, having passed the nine tests with flying colors, deserved to be the progenitor of the Jewish people. God went further, however, with a final exam, the binding of Isaac – a preparation for Isaac to be sacrificed on an altar. This was an exam so excruciating in its challenge that it remains inexplicable to this day. We can't really conceptualize why God would ask such a thing. We don't really understand why Abraham would obey. As a test, it was brilliantly devised, as it would test all three characteristics. God asked, Abraham obeyed, and the test was passed.

It is interesting to see the framing of this test as imagined by the Talmud (*Sanhedrin* 89b). Satan observed that Abraham made a major feast for the birth of Isaac (21:8) and did not offer sacrifices as part of that feast. Satan challenged God – it seems that God's favorite (Abraham) was now totally focused on his son and no longer focused on the mission. God's response was that He was so certain that Abraham remained focused on his mission that if He were to request the sacrifice of his son, Abraham would comply.

The Talmud continues that this final exam was necessary to demonstrate to all that the previous tests were valid. To further solidify how completely Abraham passed the test, the Torah reports that Abraham faithfully implemented the request even though it was expressed as a request (with the word *na*, "please") rather than as a command (22:2).

All the tests for obedience had God asking Abraham to do something difficult. Abraham needed to obey despite the difficulty. It is clear how the binding of Isaac tests obedience – and that Abraham obeyed.

Tests for belief are more challenging to analyze. As a prophet who spoke often to God, Abraham clearly believed in the Deity. We explained earlier that "belief" meant that Abraham believed that God was involved in the world and that His commitments would be fulfilled. The binding of Isaac tested that belief, because God had promised about Isaac, "I will establish My covenant with him for an everlasting covenant" (17:19). How could that be fulfilled with a request that Isaac would become a "burnt offering" (22:2)? God tested whether Abraham could go on believing under such circumstances – and he passed that test as well.

Lastly, test 10 also challenged Abraham's ability to fulfill his mission of establishing a faith community anchored in his family. Without Isaac to carry on the mission, the mission would fail. Could Abraham continue the mission despite the shock of God's request? In the end, although God put him to the test, Abraham did not slow down.

In this chapter, we have supported our thesis that obedience, belief, and commitment to transmission are the key qualifications for Abraham and the Chosen People. The ten tests that God prepared for Abraham tested precisely for those characteristics. The one that is explicitly called a test in the Torah (22:1) in fact was the final exam and tested for all the attributes.

We also further understand the purpose of the biblical narrative. We now understand the particular selection of vignettes chosen to describe Abraham's life in chapters 12–22 of Genesis. These are not random events in his 175-year lifespan. They are the specific stories that illuminate Abraham's capabilities – and by extension the qualifications of the Chosen People.

Chapter 3

More on the Chosen People

Our purpose in this book is to explore the flow of Genesis chapters 12–28, so we began by discovering that the Torah's purpose was to identify the characteristics of the Chosen People. Also, we discussed how Abraham was tested to show his worthiness. In the preface, however, we began with more fundamental questions, such as why there is a separate Chosen People. Before speculating on that question, we needed to establish the core purpose of the text – to establish and test for the qualifications.

With that behind us, we can now explore the broader question. Specifically, did God always plan to have a Chosen People? After all, in today's egalitarian world, it does not seem logical that one nation should be designated as such. We could not address that question until now. Without knowing the mission of the Chosen People, how could one possibly understand the motivation for creating such a clan?

A related question is to understand the timing of the selection of Abraham. In the biblical narrative, the world had existed for thousands of years before Abraham was selected. Why wait so long? What was the particular set of events that made this time appropriate?

The goal of this chapter is to address these questions, in the course of which we will explain additional parts of Genesis. For example, Genesis chapter 14 seems like an overly long and detailed description of some war. Why is that needed in the Torah? We will see that it is a major clue about the timing and purpose of the selection of the Chosen People.

Did God Always Plan to Choose a People?
In the first chapter of Genesis, the world was created without a Chosen People. But the Midrash (*Bereishit Rabbah* 1) says that God looked into the Torah and created the world. Given that the Torah has a dual system – seven

Noahide laws for everyone and 613 mitzvot for Jews – one might infer that
the notion of a Chosen People was foreordained.

But that is not necessarily the case. It could be that God's original plan was
to create the world with seven mitzvot for all of mankind. Then, at a later
time, when mankind became more sophisticated, God would teach the full
Torah to everyone. In other words, one could imagine a plan wherein there
would never be a distinction between nations.

But if that were God's plan, how could it be that He would change His
mind? Wouldn't omniscient God know whether that vision would work out?
We can't really comprehend the idea that God's plans could change, but in the
writings of our Sages, we see room for this idea.

The Midrash (*Bereishit Rabbah* 3:7) says that prior to the creation of our
world, God was "*Borei olamot u'Machrivan.*" That means there were numerous worlds that preceded ours. God would create a world and destroy it, then
attempt it again with a different world. What was God doing with those
worlds? Apparently imagining a world, creating it, placing some uncertainty
into that world (e.g., free will), and seeing how it turned out. Seemingly, He
was dissatisfied with the results.

What does it *really* mean when we say that God created and destroyed
numerous worlds? What were these worlds? We don't really know. Is this a
reference to other life forms on Earth? Is this a reference to life in other parts
of the universe? Does this mean that there were different universes that were
created before ours? We don't know, and we don't care. For our purposes, the
main conclusion is that God might set up some world, destroy it, and create a
better one in its place with different assumptions. This opens up the theoret-
ical possibility that God places some uncertainty into His worlds.

There is a Midrash brought by Rashi (1:1, s.v. "*bara Elokim*") in which he
notes that the language of 1:1 implies the world was created with the stern
godly attribute of "judgment." But Rashi also points out that in 2:4, it is
implied that God created the world both with judgment and with the attribute of "mercy." Rashi concludes that God had originally intended to create
the world with judgment, saw that the world could not possibly survive, and
decided instead to create the world with both judgment and mercy. Whatever
that may mean in detail, it again suggests some notion of God changing His
plans and experimenting with models of the world.

Aside from these Midrashim, the Torah itself provides for the idea that God had different models of the world even within the world as we know it. God created Adam and Eve and placed them in the Garden of Eden. The experiment that Adam and Eve would lead an idyllic life failed when they ate the forbidden fruit. That's one model.

They are chased out of Paradise, and humanity lives ten generations until the deluge. A second model: the descendants of Adam and Eve were to populate the world and live ethical lives (by adhering to the Noahide laws). That failed when God saw that all but Noah had degenerated. God expresses some form of regret (6:6). The Torah reports that God sees about mankind "that every imagination of the thoughts of his heart was only evil continuously" (6:5). God destroys the second model with the deluge.

After the destruction, there is a third model, in which Noah's descendants, chastened by the deluge, should unite in leading ethical lives. God sees advantages over the second model. Man's evil inclination has moderated. It is now only "evil from his youth" (8:21), rather than "only evil" (6:5). God is sufficiently moved by this better model of mankind that He promises never again to destroy mankind (9:15). This is a major vow from a God Who previously had created and destroyed worlds. In this third model, there is no Chosen People. Quite the contrary, this was a united population with a single language (11:1). That is the antithesis of a Chosen People. The third model was potentially destined to be the new permanent model. With a common language, all people were to unite in the worship of God (see Kli Yakar 11:1). Perhaps at some point, they would be given 613 mitzvot. But then, something bad happened (11:4). Misguided leaders took the unity and used it to attack God. That led to the Tower of Babel and the dispersion.

Reviewing the history – that God created and destroyed numerous worlds and that Genesis describes three models in the first eleven chapters (Garden of Eden, antediluvian, postdiluvian) – we can clearly see that the concept of a Chosen People was not God's only possible plan.

The Need for a Chosen People

Let's continue to analyze God's options, so to speak, after the dispersion.

After the deluge, God had promised (8:21) to never again destroy the world, and there was a reduction in the level of evil in the world. Perhaps the deluge was sufficient reminder to mankind that they needed to unify to do good. But then came the Tower of Babel and the dispersion. The Torah reports that this third model for running the world was not working.

Since mankind did not unify for good, but God promised not to destroy mankind, it was presumably not God's intent to leave humanity in a perpetually degraded state. God decided on the dispersion as the appropriate punishment for the generation of the Tower of Babel. But punishment by itself does not establish a world with proper behavior. God would not want to replace the Babel culture – in which everyone sinned in one place and in one language – with a new culture in which people would be dispersed and sin in multiple places in multiple languages. What problem would that solve?

To address this, God created a mission. There would be a person who would become a *nesi Elokim* (23:6) – a prince of God. He would be the progenitor of a Chosen People. The person's mission and the mission of the nation he would sire would be identical. They would lead a life of devotion to God. A life of obedience. God would bring them closer by providing additional commandments to them. They would be a constant reminder to all nations of the world that our purpose is to lead ethical lives, being a credit to God.

Beyond obedience, God also insisted that this nation would believe in the ethical plane of creation. God created a world with purpose. God is involved in this world, rewarding, punishing, and fulfilling commitments.

Implied by this mission is that neither the designated person nor the nation would lead monastic, separated existences. Instead, they would be integrated into the world so they could demonstrate godliness throughout it. Abraham is referred to as a prince of God *b'tocheinu* (23:6) – "among us."

This is a plausible explanation why identifying a Chosen People became God's plan with the failure of the third model for the world. This people would *transmit* widely to the world about God's ethical values and would obey them. This demanding set of 613 commandments would not be required of everyone, but seeing this Chosen People would inspire the rest of humanity to obey the basic seven Noahide laws.

Through this lens, the Jewish people's various exiles can be seen as requirements of our mission – the need to demonstrate godliness to the four corners of the earth. God told Abraham that the cauldron that creates nationhood would be an exile in a foreign land (15:13). Perhaps the exile after the Second Temple (70 CE) was required to spread God's word everywhere. One might equally say that the current ingathering into the State of Israel can be explained by modern mobility, travel, and communications technology, as we no longer need to be in the four corners of the earth to spread the ethical message of Judaism.

God establishes this as the mission from the very beginning of chapter 12. He asks Abraham to move to Canaan, where He will make him into a great and blessed nation. But the conclusion of this mission statement is "and in you shall all families of the earth be blessed" (12:3). This is not a personal mission for Abraham to achieve personal greatness. It is also not a national mission for the Chosen People to achieve insular national greatness. That may happen too, but that is not God's purpose. God's purpose is the redemption of the entire world.

From the outset, God communicates that the purpose of the Chosen People is to repair the world. This provides further evidence that God decided on having a Chosen People as a way of recovering from the evils of Babel.

Timing of the Selection
In the Genesis chronology, there were nearly two thousand years of civilization without a Chosen People. When exactly did God decide to have a Chosen People?

The Torah is building up to a crescendo about the need to change the model of the world. The first three models were tried and were found around the time of the dispersion to be wanting. Had they succeeded, perhaps there would not have been a need for a Chosen People at all. The world existed for many years before God identified Abraham. But at the failure of the third model, He begins to search for a Chosen People. The world migrates to a model in which the Chosen People play a unique role to ensure that God's messages and ethical values are accepted globally.

According to *Seder Olam*, Abraham was forty-eight years old at the time of the dispersion after the Tower of Babel. He was seventy at the Brit bein Habesarim (Genesis chapter 15; see also Chizkuni 15:7) and seventy-five when he left Charan (Genesis chapter 12). (Note that according to *Seder Olam*, the events described in Genesis chapter 15 took place prior to those of chapter 12.) It took twenty-two years after the dispersal until the covenant with Abraham, so Abraham's selection is roughly correlated to the dispersal.

Remarkably, Abraham's mission apparently started even earlier. Above, in chapter 1, we cited the Talmud, *Avodah Zarah* 9a. That discussion described that Abraham had begun to teach the ways of God at age fifty-two. It seems that after the dispersion, Abraham immediately started to pick up the pieces and guide the world to Torah. So he was demonstrating qualifications at exactly the time when God decided to begin searching for the Chosen People.

It is interesting to look at the commentary of the Tiferes Yisrael on Ethics of the Fathers 5:2. The Mishnah relates that there were ten generations from Noah to Abraham. Since these generations angered God, Abraham received the reward of all of them. The Tiferes Yisrael explains that God's plan had been to reward all of humanity with closeness to God (covenant, Torah, etc.). When they sinned, this inheritance went only to Abraham and the Jewish people. Apparently, this is a clear opinion that the decision to have a Chosen People resulted from mankind exercising their free will to sin. Had they behaved differently, all people would have been included in the covenant at some point in time.

According to this understanding, the Tower of Babel is the event that destroys the third model and determines the rough timing of the beginning of the Chosen People. Although the descendants of Noah were less sinful than their earlier counterparts, they still lacked the positive unity to carry out God's wishes. They unified *against* God and then descended into a set of warring states – each with their own set of values and false deities. God needed a fourth model. At that moment, what was He to do?

One thing that God could not do was start over. He had made the commitment to Noah not to destroy the world. Large numbers of nations with generally evil inclinations were going to be the norm on the planet. Going forward, there would be one nation – a worthy nation that would be a light unto the nations. This nation would be close to God by having a higher degree of religious obligation. Other nations would see this but would not be required to fulfill the larger quantity of mitzvot. Having the Chosen People observe this higher level of obligation would be a constant reminder to humanity of God and His commandments. The existence of a model nation would focus everyone on adhering, at a minimum, to the Noahide laws. People could convert to Judaism if they wished – but it was not a requirement.

There is no hard proof in the text for the causality between the evils of the Tower of Babel and the decision to have a Chosen People. But the flow of the text supports this. Chapters 10 and 11 of Genesis are the backdrop to chapter 12. The timing of Abraham's selection and his mission were not arbitrary. After the dispersion of chapter 11, God found someone worthy – and decided it was time to start having a Chosen People. Chapter 11 explains the generations that led to Abraham. Abraham's mission was part of a larger story as God continued to refine His model for the world.

The timing also relates to the discussion in chapter 1 about Shem and Ever. The traditional date for the Tower of Babel and the dispersion is 1996 BCE – 340 years after the deluge. At that time, Shem – who was born before the flood – was an old man. Even Ever, who was born within a hundred years after the flood, was an old man at the time of the dispersion. When God decided to look at a new spiritual model for civilization, He wanted to find a new leader.

Both Shem and Ever were senior members of society at the time of the dispersion. Despite their greatness, they were unable to provide the leadership required to be princes of God amidst the nations. Perhaps they were great scholars or pious individuals fulfilling God's commandments. But that did not mean that they were at the level of Abraham, who could be an influencer of society at large (see Radak 11:1, s.v. "*devarim achadim*"). Ever prophetically knew of the dispersion (Rashi 10:25, s.v. "*niflegah*") but was powerless to stop the events that would cause it. All of this contributed to Abraham being the superior selection.

Interestingly, Shem (and possibly Ever) continue to represent the Jewish people to this day. Jews are known to be Semitic people (the term deriving from the name Shem). More ominously, Jew haters are called anti-Semites. Jews are also called Hebrews, which is a word derived from the name Ever ("Ivri" in Hebrew; see Radak 14:13).

When the Torah is read weekly in the synagogue, the chapters up through Genesis 11 and the chapters starting at Genesis 12 are read in different weeks. That obscures the causality of this progression of the Torah's vignettes. But since chapter 12 is sequenced right after chapter 11, a connection is plausible.

To be sure, it was not sufficient to be alive at the right time to be chosen. Indeed, Abraham was also worthy. He transmitted the word of God to others. He let himself be thrown into a fiery furnace for denying idolatry. And he had the qualifications of obedience, belief, and commitment to transmission.

The Mission of the Chosen People

We see a clear thread from the beginning of Genesis. Genesis is the story of God explaining the cosmology that links the Jewish people with God and the people of the world.

In *Genesis: A Torah for All Nations*, we explained how the Torah developed expectations for all mankind in chapters 1–11 of Genesis. But through the forbidden fruit, the deluge, and the Tower of Babel, the Torah also describes how difficult it was to anchor the proper behavior of mankind. God tried various approaches. As mankind proved itself lacking, God determined the ultimate model. A Chosen People committed to obedience, belief, and transmission would model proper behaviors and ultimately establish baseline norms for the entire world. This then becomes the mission of the Chosen People – to implement the ideas that qualified them for the task of being the Chosen People.

Through a series of covenants (such as Noah 9:9), God established that He would no longer create and destroy worlds. With Abraham and the Patriarchs, He established additional covenants and blessings to finalize that the Chosen People model was the ultimate everlasting model to which He – and we – are committed (17:7).

After establishing an everlasting covenant with Abraham, at the end of the Torah, God repeats the covenant with the Jews preparing to enter Israel. In Deuteronomy, the Torah says, "Neither with you only do I make this covenant" (29:13). Continuing, God specifies, "also with him who is not here with us this day" (29:14), which Rashi explains to mean future grandchildren.

Communicating the Fourth Model

When God ends the first model of the world – casting Adam and Eve out of Eden – there is a clear statement that Adam and Eve must remake their lives in a new setting (3:23–24). When God brings the deluge to end the second model of the world, there is a long description (chapters 6–8) about how

God brings destruction but then is pleased by Noah's behavior (8:21). We have argued that there is a transition from the third model (unified mankind) to the fourth model (Chosen People). We see this gradually. First, there is the dispersion to end the third model. But the fourth model does not begin immediately.

There is a gradual emergence of the Chosen People. But the causality between the dispersion and the Chosen People is less direct. Can we find in the Torah a vignette that is the tipping point to this new model?

The battle of the kings (Genesis chapter 14) was an important event in the life of Abraham. It was one of ten tests. As discussed in chapter 2, it tested whether he would remain true to his mission despite reputation loss – which appeared to contradict God's commitment to him. It tested whether he would really believe in God's providence, given that God allowed his nephew to be captured. And at the physical level, it was both a traumatic and heroic event in Abraham's life – traumatic in that Lot was captured and heroic in that Abraham could save him.

But none of this explains the extent of the coverage or the detail. The Torah devotes an entire chapter – twenty-four verses – to this vignette. It describes Abraham's battle in excruciating detail. There must be a larger message that underlies this story.

The Sages provide subtle hints that there was an underlying importance to this vignette. We will collect those hints together and use them to describe how this battle represents the transition from the third model of the world to the model of the Chosen People. This gives an explanation of the importance of the chapter. The battle of the four kings versus the five is not a secular war. It is the defining moment of the transition to the model of the Chosen People.

It is not clear from the text who was the secular leader of mankind during the third model, but according to our Sages (Rashi 14:1), the leader was Nimrod, who is introduced to us in 10:8. Nimrod is the final representative of this third model of the world and represents the *failure* of the third model. To move forcefully to a fourth model, Nimrod needed to be taken down.

In our Sages' interpretation of the biblical narrative, Nimrod continually appears. He is the leader who commands the construction of the Tower of Babel (Rashi 10:8). He is the leader who sends Abraham into the fiery furnace for destroying idols (Rashi 11:28). And he is one of the four kings whom Abraham attacks in the battle of the kings (Rashi 14:1).

That our Sages identify one of the kings of this battle as Nimrod is an underlying message. Our Sages are not providing a mere historical footnote. There is a deeper importance to this battle that goes beyond the story of Abraham saving his nephew. This is symbolic of a greater battle between what Abraham stood for and what Nimrod stood for.

God saw that the third model – a world with one language that should unify all peoples in the worship of God – failed. He then transitioned to a fourth model, in which a particular group of people is chosen to be the ethical representative of God on earth.

By the time of the battle of the kings, Abraham has already passed three tests. Significantly, he has passed a test related to each of the three character-istics of belief, obedience, and commitment to transmission.

God has begun to upgrade His blessing to Abraham as a consequence of Abraham's passing the tests. Initially (12:2), Abraham was only promised greatness, but after the first three tests, God promised that the Land of Israel was to be Abraham's forever (13:15). God saw that His fourth model was working. He was prepared to commit that this connection was *eternal* – never to change again.

The public declaration of the new order is made as a consequence of this war. This is where God reveals to all people of that time that there has been a shift. Nimrod was first discredited when his tower project fell apart. He was minimized but not defeated. He was still a king. He threw enemies into a furnace. He subjugated weaker kings.

But in the battle of Genesis chapter 14, he was humiliated. God signaled the new world order. Ethical behaviors were blessed and successful. Evil was defeated. There would be a Chosen People starting with Abraham. That deeper story justifies the extensive length of this chapter.

Our Sages understood chapter 14 to be a giant metaphor for a world in transition. This signified the replacement of Nimrod's tyrannical power as the main force on earth with Abraham's godly devotion. This is a permanent change in the arc of history.

The demonstration of this is not only that Nimrod lost the war. There are many more details that support this hypothesis.

The four kings capture Lot (14:12). This is both a physical and a psychological capture. The physical capture is clear, the psychological one less so.

Lot is the son of Haran, who according to our Sages (Rashi 11:28) died at Nimrod's hand for rejecting idolatry. Haran, like his brother Abraham, believed in the true God, but he was not as worthy as Abraham and could not escape the grip of Nimrod. Lot, like Haran, was a believer in the true God. He left his family to join Abraham in Canaan instead of staying with his idolatrous uncle Nahor. But like his father, he was not at Abraham's level. It appeared history was about to repeat itself as he fell into the hands of his father's murderer. Would he stand up to Nimrod or succumb to idolatry? But things had changed. Abraham was ascendant. He could save his nephew. Lot's capture was setting the stage for Abraham's ascendancy. And Lot's persona, similar to that of his father Haran, was exquisitely chosen to emphasize the shift to a God-centric world.

See the contrast between the similar situations of Haran and Lot. Haran dies for not being enough of a believer. Lot is saved because he is associated with Abraham.

Abraham is informed of the capture (14:13) by a refugee from the war. Rashi identifies this refugee as Og and informs us that Og was actually a refugee from the deluge. This is surprising and requires explanation. We didn't know that there were refugees from the deluge. But more importantly, what is the message of the appearance of a "deluge refugee" in the middle of this story? Strange!

This piece of the story emphasizes God's minimization of the amoral world that preceded Abraham, to be replaced by a God-fearing world. Again, the message is to transcend the simple explanation that there was merely a physical battle. There was a battle of ideas. Nimrod aimed to be the conqueror of all. Indeed, with his tower, he had planned to do battle with God (Sforno 11:4). No one stood in his way. He was not only the ruler of this third model of the world. He was also defeating the remnants of the second model – Og. (And it's not as if Og was righteous – see Numbers 21:33.) Nimrod's power was to be absolute. But that also meant that when Abraham set out to confront this worldview, he repudiated all previous worldviews and steered the world in the path of God. Our Sages bring the tidings of Nimrod's attempted domination in the voice of an ancient warrior. Even Og had an interest in how this would turn out.

Further, when Og comes to Abraham, Abraham is referred to as the "Ivri," meaning "other side." Rashi explains that this word means that Abraham came from the other side of the river – perhaps an allusion to the fact that he had a previous run-in with Nimrod.

Then comes the most audacious part of this story. Abraham rallies his 318 trained associates to achieve what five kings could not achieve – to conquer the all-powerful four kings (14:14). What is going on? This, too, is related to the ascendancy of a God-focused world.

Rashi's explanation of this verse makes Abraham's initiative all the more remarkable. Rashi explains three key facts. Based on some numerology, Rashi concludes that Abraham did not set out with 318 associates, but rather with a single associate, Eliezer. That certainly makes the initiative even more audacious. Second, Rashi says that Eliezer is called *chanichav* (14:14), "his trained one," because Abraham taught mitzvot to Eliezer. Third, when the verse says that Abraham pursued the four kings until Dan (14:14), Rashi explains that Abraham became weak at Dan because it was a future site of idolatry of the Jewish people.

To further punctuate this drama, Chizkuni (15:2) identifies Eliezer as Nimrod's grandson. Again, we see the theme of cutting off the old world order. Even Nimrod's descendants recognized what was happening.

Taken individually, these explanations are entertaining discourse about a historical event. Taken together, however, they paint a fascinating picture.

We said that this was a battle of ideas. For a battle of ideas, Abraham does not need an army. He brings Eliezer, his most trusted confidant, whose qualification is that he is *chanichav* – he observes God's mitzvot. Abraham wages the spiritual war. But when he gets to Dan and sees that there are bleak elements in the future in terms of mitzvah observance by his future descendants, he needs to stop to catch his breath. The world is not yet fully spiritual. If idolatry returns, there is always a danger of reverting to a Nimrod world. But Abraham is victorious in the end.

The climax of the story is 14:17–20. First, in verse 17, the kings who were saved come together to greet Abraham after his victory. The place where they assemble is called the Valley of Kings. Rashi (s.v. "*emek hamelech*") explains that it was called the Valley of Kings because it was the place where the kings unanimously agreed to appoint Abraham as their overall leader. What clearer way to express that the new model of the Chosen People led by Abraham has supplanted the defeated model of Nimrod?

Further, there is a new character – a king about whom we have not heard previously – Malkizedek, the king of Salem. He is described as a priest of God. He blesses Abraham, and he blesses God. Who is Malkizedek? What does it mean that he was the king of Salem? Where was Salem? What do these three verses have to do with the rest of the story?

The way our sages explain Malkizedek supports the main message of this section. This battle represented the transition from the pre-Abrahamic world to the world in which Abraham's godliness would be the dominant value. God was ushering in the dawn of a civilization in which the Chosen People would be a guiding light for the world.

Rashi identifies Malkizedek as Shem, the son of Noah (14:18). The word *malkizedek* means the "just king." Many commentators identify Salem as Jerusalem. Rashi further explains that Shem brought out bread and wine to hint that Jerusalem is the place of holiness that will be used by Abraham's descendants as the Temple Mount and for the sacrificial order.

The interpretations of the Sages provide important tidbits about the encounter between Abraham and Malkizedek. These details come to life if one recognizes the entire chapter as a battle of ideas and the shift to a God-oriented world under the spiritual leadership of Abraham.

After winning the battle of ideas, Abraham goes to the holiest place on earth, the Temple Mount in Jerusalem. This is not a celebration of a battle on earth, but rather a coronation for God's kingship being established on earth. These verses are hinting to sacrifices. God's loyal priest celebrates the victory as a religious one.

Shem (like Og) is the connector who has seen the evolution of world orders. He witnessed the corruption of antediluvian times. He was powerless to stop the Tower of Babel and Nimrod. But now, Shem has several new roles. As the elder statesman, he anoints Abraham as the new religious leader. Shem, another survivor of the deluge, had carried his father's spiritual mantle to this day. He did not merit to be the forefather of the Chosen People, but he was still dedicated to the service of God. His blessing, therefore, is the capstone of Abraham's assumption of leadership. His public calling out of Abraham's leadership brings the attention of the entire world to the Chosen People. And this leadership is acknowledged by the other kings.

Tests, Blessings, and Ascending the Ladder

Chapter 14 of Genesis is the clarion call that the progenitor of the Chosen People has been chosen, there will be a Chosen People with a unique mission, and the third model of the world yields to this new model for bringing ethical values into the world.

While Genesis chapter 14 calls this out clearly, its placement in the middle of the ten tests is odd. If you look carefully at the ten tests and the various blessings and covenants established between God and Abraham, this chapter is just one step along a ladder of selection. As Abraham passes more tests, the commitments made to him progressively increase.

Going deeper, it is interesting to speculate when the choice of Abraham was actually finalized. On the one hand, it seems that God selected him at the beginning of Genesis chapter 12. But on the other hand, that was before the ten tests. What was the point of the tests if he had already been definitively chosen? It seems that Abraham's selection was *not* finalized at the beginning of chapter 12. Rather, he was merely *selected to be a candidate* for the role of Patriarch. As the Ramban explains (15:18), God initially only directed Abraham to go to a new land where he would become great (12:1–2). Abraham needed to accumulate merits before he could get the full blessings that were designated for the Chosen People. Genesis describes a process for Abraham to prove that he was worthy – and in that process, God incrementally provided more promises to Abraham.

The difference between being a candidate for founding Patriarch or being chosen for the job is enormous. It clarifies that the Genesis narrative is the qualification procedure. Each step along the way, Abraham moves up the ladder of selection. Ten tests must all be passed. Had he failed, we would not have a Torah that reports the failures of Abraham. Rather, God would have selected a different set of Patriarchs and Matriarchs. The Torah would have a different narrative about some other Patriarch. There would be the same immutable 613 commandments in the Torah, but with a different narrative.

This could be why other candidate Patriarchs (such as Shem and Ever) were not selected. Perhaps they were formal candidates! Maybe they were promised to become great, achieved greatness, but did not progress further. Maybe their test was to prevent the Tower of Babel. We'll never know.

We can infer that Abraham was not definitively chosen as Patriarch at the beginning of chapter 12 from the nature of his blessing there. In chapter 12, God tells Abraham to go to Canaan, where he will become a great nation (12:2). He will be a blessing (12:2). All the nations of the world will be blessed through him (12:3).

There are several items that are missing from this blessing. There is no promise about descendants. There is no promise about getting ownership of the Land of Israel. Abraham must endure the first of his tests.

Abraham passes the first test by moving to Canaan. Only then does God extend His commitment. In 12:7, God promises the land of Canaan to Abraham's descendants. God wants to see a level of success before conferring additional blessings.

Abraham passes the test of a famine, the resultant exile to Egypt, and the taking of Sarah by Pharaoh. Only after these three tests have been completed does God further extend the blessing. By then, Abraham has completed a test for each of the three crucial attributes of belief, obedience, and commitment to transmission. In chapter 13, God provides a greater commitment, promising the Land of Israel to Abraham and his descendants. Whatever distance Abraham can see will belong to Abraham's descendants forever (13:14, 15). God promises that Abraham will have descendants as numerous as the dust on the earth. That combination of promises sealed the decision that there would be a fourth and final model of God's representation in the world through the Chosen People.

That brings us to chapter 14 of Genesis as described above. At this point, God can communicate to the world that it is moving to a new model. This is a commitment forever. But we are still not done.

Abraham passed the test of the kings. That allowed him to climb additional rungs on the ladder of selection. But he must have wondered at this point how much more was left to do. On the one hand, he must have felt gratified that after test 4, God communicated that there would be a fourth model of the world. But without a descendant, what could Abraham's role be? Was he the leader of that time, introducing godly worship, only to be supplanted by some other leader at some other time? Or were the blessings of chapter 13 durable forever? This must have been confusing, given his lack of progeny.

That caused enough fear in the heart of Abraham that God needed to reassure him by saying, "Fear not, Abram" (15:1). What was the fear? Abraham confirms in 15:2, "seeing as I go hence childless." As Ramban (15:1) explains in his second explanation (s.v. "*al tira, Avram*"), Abraham was simply fearful that he would die without any children.

This is a major issue. In 15:1, God appears to him in a vision. Ramban explains that this was a higher form of prophecy. Sforno explains that God promised him everlasting reward in the World to Come. God also provides a more tangible commitment. The mere "commitment" of Genesis chapter 13 is advanced to being a "covenant" (15:18). This was apparently important to Abraham, who doubted (15:2 and 15:8) that the promise could actually be fulfilled. The promise of the land of Canaan is made more explicit with God telling him the future boundaries (15:18–21). Apparently, the land extends beyond where Abraham could walk or see. After test 4, God appears to Abraham, announcing (15:7) that He had always wanted to give the land to Abraham. Abraham asks (15:8) how he can know that this is an unconditional grant, with no strings attached. The resulting *covenant* (15:9–21) is God's guarantee that the grant is unconditional.

It is interesting to compare to Nehemiah (9:8). In that verse is a recounting that:

- God found Abraham's heart faithful ("and found his heart faithful before You").
- God made a covenant to give the Land of Israel to Abraham ("and made a covenant with him to give the land…").
- The covenant extended to Abraham's descendants ("even to give it to his seed").

The Nehemiah passage appears to link to chapter 15 of Genesis, which happens right after the test of the kings. We find the following in chapter 15:

- Abraham believed in God – i.e., his heart was faithful (15:6).
- God made a covenant to give Abraham the Land of Israel (15:18).
- The covenant extended to Abraham's descendants (15:18).

It seems that the verse in Nehemiah ties specifically to blessings after test 4.

Abraham then passes the test of taking Hagar. In chapter 17, God provides a litany of additional blessings if Abraham will undergo circumcision. With the completion of the test of Hagar and circumcisions (tests 5 and 6), Abraham has now twice passed tests related to all three of the required attributes for a progenitor: obedience, belief, and commitment to transmission. That allows him to climb additional rungs. This involves the expansion of the role of the Chosen People.

What are the additional blessings? Abram's name is changed to Abraham, signifying that he will be the father of many nations (17:5). God expresses a covenant not only with Abraham but with his descendants (17:7), as an *everlasting* covenant. Abraham has now ascended sufficiently in his qualifications that he has begun to play the critical role of influencing other nations. One may understand "father of many nations" not in the literal genetic sense, but in the sense of fulfilling his mission of demonstrating the ethical teachings of God to *all* nations. Finally, the Talmud notes (*Nedarim* 31b) that the usage of the term *brit* (covenant) thirteen times signals the importance of this new level.

There is ceremony associated with this higher level. Sforno explains that Abraham falls on his face (17:3) to signify acceptance of the growing role that the Chosen People will play and to thank God for it.

Abraham then completes the full battery of tests, including the binding of Isaac. With the completion of the tests, Abraham assumes the full role as the progenitor of the Chosen People. After the binding of Isaac, God tells him, "and in your *seed* shall all the nations of the earth be blessed" (22:18). Recall that in Genesis chapter 12, Abraham was advised only that he would be a blessing to the nations of the world. The commitment that his *descendants* will also fulfill this mission is its ultimate completion – he is to be the Patriarch of the Chosen People.

In chapter 7, we explain that the testing of the Patriarchs was not complete with Abraham. Otherwise, all of Isaac's descendants (e.g., Esau) would have been included in Abraham's covenant. Apparently, even though Abraham's and Sarah's descendants would not all be included in the Chosen People, God somehow knew that Abraham and Isaac had reached the point of no return – they would be progenitors of the Chosen People.

In the introduction, we wondered why unlike Noah and Moses – whose greatness was lauded when they were introduced in the Torah – Abraham gets his mission without prior mention of his greatness. We now understand the reason. Noah established his full measure of righteousness prior to being chosen. He was hundreds of years old when God decided on the deluge. Moses was "good" from birth and did good deeds in his formative years. Much later – at age eighty – he was called on to deliver the Jews from Egypt.

But Abraham's pattern is different. He was a pious individual when he was selected as a candidate for the patriarchal mission. But he was still untested. His true qualifications needed to be verified in a process that was interleaved with his assent to the patriarchal role. Characterizing his worthiness had to wait until later in the storyline.

We have explained that there was an interleaving of testing and blessings. Appendix 2 maps this out with charts that both enumerate the tests and blessings and provide interpretations of how the testing yielded a greater fulfillment of the selection of the Chosen People.

Chapter 4

Sarah and the Matriarchs

The narrative in these chapters is predominantly a conversation between God and Abraham. The Torah narrates the story of Abraham and Sarah as if Abraham alone is the primary prophet. God talks to Abraham, not Sarah. Abraham is the more active partner in most of the vignettes.

But as we discussed above, Abraham did not perform his mission as a personal lonely mission. It was a joint mission together with his wife Sarah, with the goal of launching a family mission and ultimately a national mission. Sarah was the indispensable partner.

This more prominent role exhibited by the Patriarchs leads to the question of how our Sages saw the role of the Matriarchs. In this chapter, we will develop the role of Sarah as seen through the eyes of our Sages. The Sages had an egalitarian view, ascribing tremendous worth to Sarah. Sarah and Abraham are equal founding partners for the Chosen People. We will support this assertion by reference to verses of Genesis and by tying it in with the three key characteristics and ten tests.

A deep discussion of the role of the Matriarchs can be found in *Abraham's Journey: Reflections on the Life of the Founding Patriarch*, by Rabbi Joseph B. Soloveitchik (KTAV, 2008). In that book (page 192), the Rav expresses Sarah's centrality as follows: "The originator of the covenant and creator of a new moral code was not a single individual. Two people were charged with the task, a man and a woman, Abraham and Sarah. They were both indispensable for the implementation of the divine plan. Both of them connected people; both taught the way. Once Sarah died, Abraham's assignment came to an end."

Sarah's Personal Characteristics

Sarah is introduced to us in 11:29. Rashi comments that her nickname was Iscah and provides three derivations for this name.

1. She could see with *ruach hakodesh* (divine inspiration).
2. All looked at her beauty.
3. She was royal.

The first point – her prophetic ability – is emphasized later in the narrative. In 21:12, after Sarah demands the expulsion of Hagar and Ishmael, God tells Abraham to listen to Sarah. Rashi explains that we see that Sarah's prophetic abilities were superior to Abraham's. As our Sages developed their approach to Sarah, they not only emphasized the equality of Abraham and Sarah, but in some aspects lauded Sarah even above Abraham.

The derivation of the name Iscah might also be related to "anointing." With that interpretation, Sarah could see with divine inspiration, as if she had been anointed with that ability.

Her beauty and her royal nature are not spiritual attributes, but they point to her as a natural leader. Her beauty, which is noted explicitly elsewhere (e.g., 12:11, 14), might be viewed as a superficial quality. But interestingly, Ethics of the Fathers (6:8) identifies beauty as a desirable quality for the righteous and those they interact with – presumably because it attracts others to the cause. Similarly, having a royal upbringing or demeanor is a positive quality. Not only is the name Iscah indicative of royalty, but the name Sarah also derives from the root *sar*, meaning "official" or "prince."

We see praise of Sarah's qualities at her death. The Torah reports her age at death (127 years) as a hundred years and twenty years and seven years (23:1). Rashi interprets that long description as praise. Even when she reached a hundred, she was without sin as a twenty-year-old (since a twenty-year-old cannot be viewed as fully responsible), and her beauty was like that of a seven-year-old. The theme of beauty is repeated, and the attribute of being without sin is added.

Sarah's Name Change

In 17:5, as part of a covenant with Abraham, God changes his name from Abram to Abraham, adding an extra letter (*heh*) to his name. This is the introduction to the covenant of circumcision. God is explicit that the reason for this name change is that Abraham will be the forefather of many nations.

Rashi (17:5) adds that the sound of the new name, Abraham, sounds like "father of many nations."

The treatment is shockingly different several verses later when God informs Abraham that Sarah's name will change from Sarai to Sarah (17:15). The Torah is understated in the change of name. Sarah is not told directly; instead, God tells Abraham. The Torah does not give any reason for this name change.

Despite the parsimony of words, our Sages don't see a difference in message between Abraham and Sarah. Rashi is explicit. The name Sarai means "Abraham's princess." The name Sarah means "princess over all people." In other words, the added letter plays the same role for Sarah as it does for Abraham. It extends their mission from being a local mission within their own clan and makes them role models for the entire world. This is consistent with the mission that Abraham and Sarah saw for themselves, as discussed in chapter 1.

Rabbi Samson Raphael Hirsch takes it a step further. He not only extols Sarah based on the change of name. He says that the change of name is to ensure that we understand that Sarah has status. Specifically, he points out that until 17:15, the Torah focuses only on Abraham, the male, as a participant in the covenant. Here, Sarah is called upon in equal worthiness and importance. The equality is signaled because just as Abraham is "upgraded" by the change of his name, so too is Sarah.

As we discussed above, remarkably, Abraham does not even focus on Sarah's name change. There is no evidence that he mentions to Sarah that she has been blessed – that only shows up when the angels appear in chapter 18 and Sarah overhears the message. Instead, he broods about why Ishmael cannot also be part of the covenantal family. We explained above that this is because of Abraham's expansive view of his mission to embrace his entire family. No disrespect is intended for Sarah. Yet it is another example of the Sages coming back to ensure that Sarah's credit is clear even when she is not directly elevated by the Torah narrative.

Sarah and the Three Qualifications

Abraham was qualified as the progenitor of the Chosen People because he had the three attributes of obedience, belief, and commitment to transmission. Did Sarah share those attributes?

We know Abraham possessed those qualities because we found three verses where God extolled Abraham for having them. We also discussed in chapter 2 how the tests verified that Abraham indeed had those attributes (and we'll see below that some of that applied to Sarah). But other than the tests, can we find in the text or in the writings of our Sages that Sarah had the three attributes? Certainly, there are no three explicit passages in the Torah as we found for Abraham.

Looking at the evidence, we can see that our Sages understood that Sarah had the three qualifications. We already quoted Rashi (12:5) that even in Charan, Sarah converted the women to follow God's path. *Commitment to transmission* is clearly noted by our Sages.

Obedience can be understood at two levels. At the most basic level, it means that the individual obeys the will and law of God. Evidently, if Sarah was converting others to do so, she was certainly behaving in the right way herself.

But obedience in our context means something deeper. In those tests that were focused on obedience, displaying that quality meant that Abraham and Sarah would do what God asked, even under treacherously difficult circumstances. While there is no declaration in the text that Sarah was "obedient" as there was for Abraham (22:18), we will see in the next section that Sarah was challenged by these tests and succeeded as well.

It is interesting to discuss whether Sarah had the characteristic of *belief* that was required. At one level, since she had a higher prophetic ability than Abraham (see the first section of this chapter), she must have believed in God. But as we discussed in chapter 2, belief does not simply mean belief in God. It means belief that God is involved in and caring about the world and that He will fulfill his commitments.

It is somewhat difficult to assess whether Sarah had this belief, because we don't know what commitments God made to her. God made many commitments to Abraham, including the birth of Isaac (first in 17:19 and again in Genesis chapter 18). Did Abraham tell Sarah? When did she first find out?

Recognizing that Sarah was at a higher prophetic level than Abraham, we might assume that Sarah knew about her destiny to have a child. Although she knew about that destiny, she might have doubted that God would fulfill the commitment. But she, like Abraham, believed without doubt that God would fulfill the commitment.

Here is a more specific example. While it took time for her to have a child, she took steps to facilitate that result. At age sixty-five, she traveled with Abraham to a new land. At the age of seventy-five, Sarah asked Abraham to take Hagar (16:2). According to some commentaries (see Sforno), Sarah thought that this would lead to having her own child from Abraham. The fact that she took proactive steps at age seventy-five indicates that she had a belief that the commitment would be fulfilled.

And, after Isaac was born, she made it a point to advertise to the world that the birth was a clear signal that God keeps His commitments (21:7; also see Rashi and his grandson the medieval commentator Rashbam).

Sarah's Tests

We discussed in the last chapter why there was an imperative to test whether Abraham had the qualifications to be the progenitor of the Chosen People. Above, we argued that it was equally important for Sarah to have the same qualifications. Presumably, she also needed to be tested. Let's look at the collection of tests and see how they applied to her.

We will see that she was involved in many of the tests. She was not involved in all, so God apparently didn't need to test her ten times. On the other hand, arguably, some of the tests actually tested Sarah more than they did Abraham. That may compensate for her having fewer tests. Going through the first nine of the tests, we have:

1. Departing Charan to move to Canaan. This tested *both* of them. Since Sarah did not have a direct conversation with God as Abraham did, one could argue that it was a *greater* test for her. She needed to move without knowing firsthand that it was a divine command.
2. Famine. This tested *both* equally.
3. The taking of Sarah to Pharoah. This tested Sarah *more greatly* than it tested Abraham. If a disaster had happened and Pharoah had held on to Sarah, she would have lost everything in terms of her ability to be a transmitter and part of the progenitor family. Abraham, though, could have continued with his mission.

4. The battle of the four kings versus the five. Involvement in the military conflict seemed to involve Abraham more. On the other hand, the family member who was captured in the conflict was Lot – Sarah's brother.
5. Abraham's taking of Hagar. Although this action was actually suggested by Sarah, given the circumstances, it seems it was a *greater* test to Sarah.
6. Circumcision at age ninety-nine. This did *not* test Sarah.
7. The king of Gerar takes Sarah. As in test 3, this appears to be a *greater* test of Sarah.
8. God commands to send away Hagar. This appears to be a test primarily of Abraham.
9. The expulsion of Ishmael. This appears to test Abraham.

Of these nine tests, it appears that three tested Sarah even more than Abraham (3, 5, and 7), two tested them roughly equally (1 and 2), one tested Abraham somewhat more (4), and three do not appear to test Sarah at all (6, 8, and 9). Overall, Sarah does not appear to be tested as frequently as Abraham, but she indeed is tested. Compensating for when she is not tested are circumstances where her test is a greater challenge.

We also see that Sarah received testing for all three characteristics. She was tested for obedience (1), belief (2 and 4), and commitment to transmission (3, 5, and 7).

The tenth test – the binding of Isaac – is most interesting.

At first glance, Sarah is not involved. The entire episode involves Abraham, Isaac, and two lads who accompany the journey. In this most pivotal test – the final exam, which tests everything all together – Sarah is not part of the effort.

Our Sages, however, do link Sarah into the story in a curious fashion. Rashi (23:2, s.v. "*lispod*") quotes the Midrash, which explains the circumstances of Sarah's death. Sarah learned about the binding and near-death of Isaac, and that bad tiding caused her soul to escape from her body, causing her death.

It is interesting to speculate what the Midrash is trying to teach us. It certainly could be logical that a 127-year-old woman would be shocked to hear what Abraham did with Isaac. Indeed, it could be shocking enough to cause death. But is the Midrash merely trying to tell us about a physical reaction of the foundational greats of the world? Torah messages tend to have moral lessons behind them.

It seems the Midrash is tying Sarah into the tenth test. She is not a direct actor in the event – so she is not tested directly. In some sense, she is the victim; she is not exposed to the entire intrigue of how the test is developed and executed. God issues a direct command, Abraham follows the command, God saves Isaac. Her involvement is simply to react when the entire story is told to her in one instant.

So that is her test. Does her death indicate that she somehow did something improper? Or did she die for some other reason?

What exactly was being tested? Since she was not commanded in the binding, it was not her obedience that was being tested. Since she was not asked to cut off the path of transmission as Abraham had been, it was not her commitment to transmission that was being tested. It was her belief. God required that the Patriarchs and Matriarchs had unquestioned belief in God fulfilling His commitments.

We can ask whether she passed the test: What was the expected behavior that God was looking for?

A failure of the test would have been a reaction in which she concluded that God was acting in an inappropriate or uncaring fashion. But here is how Rashi sees it (23:2, s.v. *"lispot l'Sarah"*): "her soul escaped from her body." It is not that she failed to believe – it is that her testing was over, so her soul could depart; her mission was accomplished.

Rashi brings the Midrash describing how Sarah died as an explanation of the word *lispod*, meaning "to eulogize." Rashi does not bring the Midrash to explain the circumstances of Sarah's death at the beginning of 23:2; it is brought as an explanation of the eulogy at the end of 23:2. Abraham's eulogy of Sarah – his crowning description of what Sarah accomplished in life – was that she died in response to the news of the binding. If the vignette is mentioned in the eulogy, this means it was praiseworthy. Abraham is giving testimony to Sarah's righteousness. Once Sarah heard the news, she accepted that this was an additional test from God. No more and no less. And once she passed her final exam, God peacefully took her life.

Several commentaries (e.g., Sforno 23:2) connect Sarah's death with Rebecca's birth in 22:23. Once Rebecca was born, it was safe for Sarah to pass on. Sarah saw that Isaac was saved, his wife was prepared, and the grand mission could continue with the next generation.

The continuing narrative further supports the centrality of Sarah. After Sarah's burial, the world is bereft – there is no Matriarch. Earlier, we brought Rabbi Soloveitchik's explanation that without Sarah, Abraham could not continue his mission. The immediate priority becomes to find the new Matriarch, the wife of Isaac. The Torah spends an exquisitely long sixty-seven-verse chapter 24 to describe the process of qualifying and finding the new Matriarch, Rebecca. To further support Sarah's role and righteousness, the concluding verse (24:67) reports that Isaac brought Rebecca to the tent of Sarah. Indeed, the culmination of the search was not only to find a wife for Isaac, but to find the replacement Matriarch (Rashi, ibid.).

God's Selection of Sarah

The Torah does not always present events in a linear fashion. We might have expected the story of Abraham and Sarah to begin with a grand declaration in the vein of *God called on Abraham and Sarah to be the progenitors of the Chosen People because they were worthy.* But as we saw in chapter 2, the Torah does not proceed in that manner. Genesis chapter 12 makes clear that Abraham is destined for greatness, but the reasons he is worthy are unclear.

In a similar fashion, God's selection of Sarah as the Matriarch was not introduced from the outset, but we do see later in the narrative that God selected Sarah.

It is instructive to look at 17:16–21. God informs Abraham that Sarah will have a child (17:16) who will be blessed. Abraham responds with skepticism (17:17, 18), suggesting that it was still possible that God's covenant could be established through Ishmael. God rejects this suggestion. God is explicit that the line of succession comes from Sarah – not from Hagar. The all-important covenant into which God has entered with Abraham only goes through Isaac (17:19, 21). True, God will bless Ishmael (17:20), and he will be great. But greatness is not covenant. It is not the opportunity to lead the Chosen People. That goes only through the Sarah lineage.

We see this again in the next chapter. After Abraham is informed that Sarah will have a child in Genesis chapter 17, there is no record that he ever told this to Sarah. That leads to chapter 18. We then have fifteen verses that appear unnecessary. They notify Abraham of what he was already told in

17:16 and 17:21. Why the repetition? Why the elaborate ceremony of the three angels appearing and having a meal with Abraham?

Sforno (18:9) explains that the purpose of the angelic delegation was to inform Sarah. There was no need to inform Abraham again. God was pointing to His choice of Sarah as the Matriarch.

Our Sages (*Bava Metzia* 59a) have an interesting way of expressing how Abraham was blessed by his marriage to Sarah. Based on 12:16, the Talmud concludes that from Abraham and Sarah, we see that blessing is only found in a person's home due to his wife.

Sarah's Death

Sarah is praiseworthy at her death.

Many deaths are reported in the Torah factually and unemotionally. Even Abraham's death (25:8) is reported in that way. True, the Torah describes that Abraham had a full and satisfied life and that his sons buried him in the family burial plot. But there is no emotion.

Contrast that with the elaborate story of Sarah's burial. This story takes an entire chapter, mostly dedicated to the purchase of the burial plot. But that's not all. Verse 23:2 tells that Abraham delivered a eulogy and was in tears at the event. This was no ordinary funeral. This was a great woman.

Kli Yakar explains that the terminology of the verse is strange. The verse says, "to mourn for Sarah, and to weep." But the weeping should have come first. The practice is for weeping to only last for the first three days after death, whereas mourning is for a full seven days.

He explains that ordinarily, the more intense weeping period is limited to three days because time heals. It is human nature for the intensity to lessen. In Sarah's case, the world was overwhelmingly conscious of the loss. The world was bereft of her good deeds and Torah study. That is why the weeping continued for so long.

More striking is 24:67, which is the discussion of Rebecca coming into Isaac's house as his wife. The verse states that "Isaac brought her into his mother Sarah's tent" and "Isaac was comforted for his mother." Rashi lists all the ways in which Sarah (and then Rebecca) made the home feel like a Jewish home: a lit candle, a blessing in the dough, and a cloud attached to the tent.

There was something about Sarah's tent that spoke to her special personal characteristics.

Commentaries also reflect on the last part of the verse relating to Isaac being comforted. Radak points out that Rebecca coming to Isaac took place three years after Sarah's death. Whereas mourning usually lasts a year, Isaac could not be comforted until Rebecca came. The thirteenth-century commentator Chizkuni points out that Rebecca's sharing Sarah's extraordinary good deeds caused Isaac to be comforted.

Chapter 5

Explaining Abraham's Apparent Failings

While Abraham passed the tests for obedience, belief, and commitment to transmission with flying colors, he nevertheless appeared to show questionable character traits (see appendix 1). We began the book by wondering about the purpose of this text, given that it cast Abraham in a somewhat negative light. We analyzed the text, concluding that its entire purpose was to demonstrate Abraham's qualifications, which necessitated placing him in positions of moral quandary.

But while the tests put him in a very tight spot, did he need to address the tests in a way that appeared improper? Shouldn't the narrative demonstrate irreproachable behavior? For the Torah to stand the test of time, it would be important for Abraham to demonstrate irreproachable behavior – even as people's values change in different eras.

Some of the tests did not introduce moral conflict, and Abraham's response was clear. God told him to go to Canaan, and he went. God imposed a famine, and Abraham endured it without complaint.

But some of the tests contained ethical challenges. There might not have been a clear-cut "right thing to do" – so Abraham made a choice. Here we study those choices to understand why they were correct – or at least acceptable. Some of them are hard to understand, such as encouraging a foreign ruler to take Sarah or taking Isaac to an altar.

We also discuss one vignette that is separate from the ten tests: the search for a non-Canaanite wife for Isaac (Genesis chapter 24). While that might have appeared to be acceptable to previous generations of Bible students, it could be viewed as troubling today. In today's egalitarian times, we would ask why Canaanites were inherently inferior to Arameans from Abraham's hometown.

As we look at these troublesome incidents, the intent is not to convert them into a hagiography of the Patriarchs and Matriarchs. They were human and imperfect. The Talmud itself is critical of their actions. *Baba Kamma* (93a) criticizes Sarah for complaining about Hagar and attributes Sarah's early death (at 127 years – early compared to Abraham's death) as a punishment. *Megillah* (15a) says that Abimelech cursed Abraham and Sarah for misleading him and identifies the blindness of their son Isaac (27:1) as a consequence.

But even if our forefathers were imperfect and suffered consequences due to God's exacting standards, we must identify mitigating factors that *partly* justify their actions. It is one thing to say that these luminaries were imperfect and were punished for their mistakes – that is the approach of the Talmud. It is quite another thing to read story after story about apparent missteps as a major portion of the biblical narrative.

We find a repeating pattern. It is not that Abraham's actions were wrong. Rather, the situations placed Abraham into a succession of moral dilemmas with no clear ethical solution. He makes decisions. He takes actions. They are correct. There is a path to justify his ethical choices.

In appendix 1, we identify seven vignettes that present problematic ethical choices. Four of these relate directly to tests:

- The events leading up to Sarah being taken by Pharoah (test 3, event 4 in appendix 1)
- The events surrounding Abraham's taking of Hagar (test 5, event 13)
- The events surrounding Sarah being taken by Abimelech at Gerar (test 7, event 21)
- The binding of Isaac (test 10, event 25)

In addition, there are three other tests that are tied to negative stories in lesser ways. These are:

- The battle of the kings – related to Abraham's curious separation from Lot (test 4, event 5)
- Sending away Hagar – although perhaps this was not negative because it had God's agreement (test 8, event 23)
- The expulsion of Ishmael – which also had God's agreement (test 9, events 23 and 29)

For only three of the tests – moving to Canaan (test 1), tolerating the famine (test 2), and circumcision (test 6) – was the behavior clear and beyond reproach.

Sarah, Abraham, and Pharoah

It is a struggle to understand Abraham's behavior with regard to Sarah and Pharoah.

Twice when Abraham and Sarah went into foreign lands, Sarah masqueraded as Abraham's sister so that she could be taken by the ruler of the land rather than having Abraham murdered. While the goal of protecting Abraham's life certainly makes sense, this behavior is nonetheless difficult to comprehend on many levels.

According to the Midrash, Abraham's first claim to fame (Rashi 11:28) was his willingness to be thrown into a fiery furnace rather than engage in idolatrous behavior. Abraham's character was to do what was right and stand up for his ideals no matter the result. How then can he so blithely subject his wife to adultery rather than being truthful and accept the consequences? With Pharoah of Egypt, he represents Sarah as his sister (12:11) and induces Pharoah to potentially be intimate with a married woman (12:15, 19) if not for God's interference. How could Abraham so willingly entrap Pharoah into adultery?

Further, he tries to involve Sarah in the plot. He asks her to participate in the misleading story of "we are siblings" (12:13). This makes the sin even worse. For example, if Sarah were to be taken against her will (e.g., by Egyptian conquerors), she would be considered blameless (Rambam, *Hilchot Melachim* 10:2). But by participating in the plot, she is willingly encouraging adultery!

One wonders why Abraham even went to Egypt. True, there was a famine (12:10), and many commentaries (e.g., Rashi) explain that this was a test. Abraham was being tested as to whether he would doubt God. God had promised the land of Canaan, but now new forces compelled Abraham to leave. But was it really true that Abraham was forced to leave? Commentaries explain that Abraham passed the test by leaving Canaan for Egypt and not doubting God's word. Couldn't Abraham have passed the test by staying in Canaan? God did not command him to go to Egypt; Abraham made that choice. Couldn't he have shown "belief" by staying in Canaan and believing that he would survive there? Could he not have used the considerable wealth he had brought with him (12:5) to get basic survival needs in Canaan? Indeed, Ramban (12:10) considers it a great sin that Abraham left to go to Egypt, not depending on God to save him from the famine in Israel.

In another historical epoch, Elimelech was criticized for leaving during a famine (see Rashi, Ruth 1:1). Here, too, should not Abraham have stayed?

There are other troubling aspects of this vignette. While setting up this plot, Abraham is interested in ancillary benefits. He tells Sarah that she must represent herself as his sister not only to save his life. Part of the motivation is "that it may be well with me for your sake" (12:13), which Rashi interprets to mean that the Egyptians will give gifts to Abraham. Is money so important that one sacrifices one's wife?

We have also talked about Sarah's greatness (chapter 4), so we must explain her behavior as well. She is an independent actor. She is also being tested. By going along with the plot, she is culpable if it goes awry. How is her behavior acceptable?

Based on our Sages, we provide several partial or complete explanations as to the acceptability of the behavior of Abraham and/or Sarah.

Sarah Did Not Participate in the Plot

We first dispatch, quickly, with the last question. Ramban has an interesting way to explain Sarah's behavior, but not Abraham's. After Abraham asks Sarah to lie on his behalf, there is no record that she does so. Instead, when they approach Egypt, the officers of Pharaoh praise Sarah and take her to Pharaoh. At the end of the incident, Pharaoh asks Abraham (12:19) why he lied. We can infer it was only Abraham who verbalized that Sarah was his sister. The Ramban says (12:10) that Abraham alone performed a great sin.

As a support for Sarah's lack of culpability, Radak comments (12:15) that Sarah was "taken" – meaning against her will. There is no sin in that. The Talmud (*Sanhedrin* 74b) teaches us in regard to Esther being taken by Ahasuerus that when a woman is taken by a king, regardless of the circumstances, she is not in violation of adultery because of the power imbalance between the king and the woman, who must be passive in such a relationship.

This approach frees Sarah from responsibility. Sarah was not at risk of violating the prohibition on adultery. However, this is not a strong defense of Abraham.

The rest of this section focuses on Abraham.

Why Abraham Left Canaan

When Abraham was in Ur Kasdim (see Rashi 11:28), he took an action (destroying idols) that resulted in his being thrown into a fiery furnace. If he was brave enough to face certain death at that point, why didn't he similarly face death and stay in Canaan – the Promised Land – to withstand the famine? Commentaries provide several explanations.

Radak explains the circumstances that led Abraham to go to Egypt. He would never have gone to Egypt had he known that he and Sarah would be at risk. He went thinking it would be safe. It was only when he neared Egypt (12:11) that he saw Egypt's licentious behavior. Radak argues that Abraham accidentally and without fault stumbled into the situation. Also, Radak emphasizes (12:10) that Abraham did not leave Canaan for his own sake. He had considerable cattle and people in his household, and he was responsible for their care.

Rabbi Samson Raphael Hirsch also points out that Abraham had no choice but to go to Egypt. One is not permitted to rely on a miracle if there is some other possible way out. Going to the foreign land of plenty is the required alternative, rather than expecting miraculous food to appear in Canaan. Rabbi Hirsch further says that Abraham's repetition of the behavior in Gerar (20:2), despite his bad experience in Egypt, proves it was necessary. In similar circumstances, Isaac repeats the behavior (26:7).

As to why Elimelech was criticized in similar circumstances in the book of Ruth, we can point out one key difference. Elimelech was a leader in Bethlehem and should not have demoralized the people by leaving. Abraham, as a wandering man of God, could have simply decided to move his ministry elsewhere.

How Could Lying Be Justified?

Radak (similar to Hirsch above) explains that Abraham would not rely on a miracle. Once Abraham went to Egypt and found that his own life was in danger and could only be saved with lies, it was the appropriate thing to do – in fact, the only thing to do!

By contrast, when Abraham was in Ur Kasdim (see Rashi 11:28), he destroyed idols without knowing that this would result in his being sent to a fiery furnace. He took the action and suffered the consequences. He didn't "rely" on a miracle – although God provided one to save him. In Egypt, he understood that without a lie, he faced certain death. In that case, protecting his life was preferable to telling the truth.

What about the severity of the lie? This lie is leading Pharoah to potentially commit the capital crime of adultery. Should a lie be permitted even in this case?

To see how severe adultery is, it is worthwhile to note that in Jewish law, one is permitted to violate any precept to save a life. But there are three exceptions. One exception is adultery: one may not engage in it even to save a life (Rambam, *Hilchot Yesodei Hatorah* 5:2). If adultery is so severe a transgression that you are required to lose your life rather than succumb to it, can it ever be permissible to lie in a manner that causes adultery?

There are technicalities that mitigate even such a severe lie. Let's look at it from Abraham's perspective. His life was threatened. He saw a way out by lying. The lie itself is not adultery – it is just a lie. True, it likely would lead to adultery – but that's not Abraham's problem. He is not committing the sin. It is not happening immediately. All he is doing is lying to save his life.

Further, as we have explained above, due to the power imbalance, Sarah – if forced into a relationship with Pharoah while being passive – would not be culpable for adultery.

Indeed, the Rambam writes (*Hilchot Melachim* 10:2) that if a Noahide is compelled (i.e., his life is threatened) to violate one of the seven Noahide laws, he is permitted to do so. Abraham may well be considered a Noahide, as the Torah has not yet been given at Sinai, and therefore, according to some opinions, he is not a Jew (see *Parashat Derachim, Derech Hasarim* 1, and *Beit Ha'otzar* 1). But even if he is considered a Jew, let us consider his actions from the point of view of the 613 mitzvot for the Jews. A Jew may violate a law to save his life (*Hilchot Yesodei Hatorah* 5:1–2) as long as the violation is not murder, an illegal sexual union, or idolatry. With that standard, Abraham may lie to save his life even if an indirect result is adultery. Or, as a Noahide, he could have taken the lower standard of violating any law to save his life. The Rambam is explicit (*Hilchot Melachim* 10:2) that a Noahide may even save his life by engaging in idolatry if he is compelled to do so. Again, the lie is not the illegal union itself – it is only that it has the potential to precipitate that sin.

Still, why would Abraham put Pharoah into a position of committing a capital offense? Perhaps Abraham had no choice from his own perspective. Yet to induce Pharaoh into such a grievous sin requires explanation. Indeed, Pharoah complains (12:18) that Abraham did not inform him that Sarah was married.

In *Hilchot Melachim* (10:1), the Rambam explains that if a person has relations with a married woman without knowing she is married, he is not punished. Given that in antiquity, kings had absolute power, perhaps Abraham reasoned that Pharoah – who would take Sarah in any case – was best off not knowing she was married. That way, Pharoah would not knowingly commit a capital crime.

The final question is why Abraham seemed interested in getting financial benefits. Abraham proposes the lie so that "it may be well with me for your sake, and that my soul may live because of you" (12:13). Rashi interprets "may be well" to mean that the Egyptians will send him gifts. It is hard to accept that Abraham would have such a materialistic goal, even to the point of endangering his marriage.

Abraham's behavior is better understood if we explain 12:13 according to Radak. A common literary style is to provide a message twice in one verse with different words. Radak equates "may be well with me" with "my soul may live" at the end of the same verse. In other words, the wellness that Abraham was looking for was simply that they should not kill him.

According to complex halachic analysis, Abraham's actions are explained even using the superficial meaning of the text. But there are also novel interpretations.

Abraham and Sarah Were Not Married

The above explanations (not to rely on miracles, permissibility of lying) align well with the simple letter of the text. A totally different approach to explain Abraham's behavior is provided by Rabbenu Chananel. The theory is expressed not regarding Egypt, but rather Gerar (20:2). Rabbenu Chananel says that Abraham divorced Sarah before showing up in that city. If that were the case, the "lies" were not lies at all. Sarah, daughter of Haran, was Abraham's niece (which in the local jargon could be called a sister, the word Abraham uses in 20:12), and at that point, she was not his wife. Hence there was no lie and no possibility of adultery.

The Rambam (*Hilchot Melachim* 9:8) contrasts the formal divorce proceedings under Jewish law (in which a man provides a formal writ of divorce to his wife) with how Jewish law describes divorce for Noahides. For non-Jews, the requirements are not formal. If the woman leaves her husband or he sends her off, that accomplishes divorce (somewhat akin to a common-law relationship). By declaring that Sarah must represent herself as a sister and not as a wife, Abraham was divorcing her.

This trick of divorce and remarriage could have occurred multiple times. Since Pharaoh never married her, there was no problem with Sarah's going back to Abraham. (In Judaism, if a woman remarries, she cannot later return to her first husband. That would not apply to a Noahide even if she remarried in the interim.)

Abraham Lied to Discourage Adultery

Chizkuni (12:13) has a different approach to explain Abraham's behavior. Abraham never suggested to Pharoah that the monarch should marry Sarah. In Chizkuni's view, it was never Abraham's plan that Pharoah would try to take Sarah. Quite the opposite.

Abraham suggested to Sarah that they say that she was his sister. Chizkuni posits further that they claimed that Sarah was married and her husband was far away. Abraham expected that the Egyptians would not violate a married woman. His only concern was that they were less diligent about not killing people. If Abraham were identified as the husband, he would be killed. But he expected they would not approach a woman whose husband was far away. Abraham's assumptions were wrong, but he had good intentions.

The Curious Figure of Lot

Next, let's address the appropriateness of Abraham's entire set of interactions with Lot, which includes a discussion of test 4. Abraham's behavior toward

Lot reveals a mix of reactions. Some of the interactions, such as their separation in Genesis chapter 13, seem questionable. We need a complete understanding of Lot and his relationship with Abraham.

Lot starts out as a "good guy." When Abraham sets out for Canaan, the Torah tells us twice that Lot went with him (12:4–5). The first "and Lot went with him" indicates that Lot was eager to come on the mission (see Chizkuni).

The falling out happens in 13:6–9. Their mutual wealth caused strife between their herdsman (13:7). Abraham resolves the strife by suggesting that they separate. Each will move to a separate land so that they can thrive without strife. Superficially, this is a logical way to solve the dispute.

But it is unsatisfactory. Abraham's mission in life was not to accumulate wealth, it was to be perfect in the eyes of God (17:1). Lot apparently was a partner in this. Could they not have found an amicable way to continue their relationship? Lot had come so far with Abraham; could a mere quarrel among their employees be a cause for separation?

And if there were to be separation, the path that they chose was extreme. Abraham was in Bethel, a city north of Jerusalem. Lot chose to move to Sodom (13:12), a city south of the Dead Sea. That is a distance of more than 100 kilometers. This was not a minor separation to repair a small quarrel.

Further, the Torah reports that Sodom was an evil city (13:13). In reaction to this small quarrel, was there no better solution than for Abraham to send Lot into this den of iniquity? Is that the proper treatment of the loyal nephew who accompanied Abraham from so far away?

This relates to test 4. Lot being captured was a long-term consequence of Abraham's pushing Lot out of his life (13:9), whereupon Lot went to the terrible city of Sodom. Couldn't Abraham have prevented this entire episode with better treatment of Lot?

To understand the relationship between Lot and Abraham, we need to go back to the beginning and assess their entire relationship.

Lot plays an outsized role in the early days of Abraham's ministry. He travels with Abraham to Canaan (12:4, 5), apparently also goes with Abraham to Egypt and then to the Negev (13:1), quarrels with Abraham (13:5–9), and moves to Sodom (13:10–13). The inclusion of the twenty-four verses of chapter 14 – the war of the nine kings – is apparently caused by Lot's capture. While the story of the destruction of Sodom and Gomorrah is an important story in its own right, the thirty-eight verses of chapter 19 place Lot into the central focus of that narrative.

Who was Lot? What was his story? Why was it so important to include in the Torah? Generally, Lot is viewed unfavorably because of his actions in Genesis chapter 19. Ohr Hachayim (12:1) states that when God commanded Abraham to leave his father's house, he was supposed to leave Lot behind. But Abraham either didn't understand God's command or couldn't follow through, because Lot stuck to Abraham. Then Abraham found the flimsiest excuse (13:9) to place significant distance between himself and Lot.

The full story must be more complex. Much of Abraham's life is dedicated to excellent treatment of Lot. Abraham saved him in the battle of the kings and argued on his behalf at the destruction of Sodom. Lot was more than a hanger-on.

Let's recall the biographical facts. Terah had three sons: Abraham, Haran, and Nahor (11:26). Haran had three children: Lot (11:27), Milcah (11:29), and Iscah (11:29). Our Sages identify Iscah as Sarah (Rashi 11:29).

Terah and Nahor were idolators (Rashi 31:53). Abraham believed in God and for that was thrown into the fiery furnace by King Nimrod (Rashi 11:28). Haran was a good man, but not good enough. When he saw Abraham exit from the fiery furnace, Haran declared his allegiance to God. He was thrown into the furnace. Since he was not as worthy as Abraham, he died (Rashi 11:28).

Just as Terah had three children – the good (Abraham), the bad (Nahor), and the one with some potential to be good (Haran) – it seems that Haran's children had the same pattern. Sarah was good, and Milcah was presumably bad (she married Nahor).

That leaves us with Lot. When Abraham went on the mission to the land of Canaan, Lot eagerly went with him. He could have stayed with Nahor in his birthplace. That would have been most comfortable. Why did he go on this arduous journey? It seems that he was persuaded that the path of his uncle and aunt/sister (Abraham and Sarah) was the right path. He aligned with the better nature of his father Haran.

We see that in the language of the Torah. When it reports that Abraham left for Canaan, it specifies twice that Lot went with him. It is reported in 12:5 that Abraham *took* Sarah and Lot, but it is reported in 12:4 that Lot *went* – apparently voluntarily – with Abraham. Chizkuni (12:4) points out that since Haran had died, Lot was a member of Abraham's household. He was Abraham's ward.

From Abraham's perspective, Lot was destined to be part of the great nation that God promised to him (12:3). In the initial blessing given to Abraham prior to emigrating, there was no mention yet that Abraham was starting a *hereditary* dynasty. This is presumably why Abraham and Sarah brought all their converts with them (12:5). Even when God promised the land to Abraham's descendants (12:7), there was no mention that converts would be excluded. As we know to this day, converts to Judaism are accepted with open arms. There was every reason to believe that Lot would become part of the Chosen People.

Lot continues to be with Abraham in a positive light in Egypt. In Deuteronomy (2:5), Rashi explains that Lot was praiseworthy because he did not reveal to Pharoah that Sarah was Abraham's wife. There was peace until the rivalry between their respective shepherds, so it is important to examine that rivalry carefully.

Significantly, it is not an argument between Abraham and Lot. They are on the same page. Abraham approaches Lot to resolve the argument and suggests that they find an amicable solution, "because we are brothers" (13:8).

What happens next?

Evidently, somewhere between chapter 13 and chapter 19, something happens with Lot. By the time we get to chapter 19, Lot may still be worthy of saving, but he is no longer leading a life of saintliness. The Sages (e.g., Ramban 19:8) point out numerous actions done by Lot that suggest an underlying level of immorality.

When did Lot change? He probably was not evil while living with Abraham. If he always wanted to be evil, he would have stayed with Nahor in Charan. Did he sour on the religious mission as soon as he left Abraham? Or was it the length of time in Sodom that finally caused his standards to deteriorate?

It is interesting to trace the development through the eyes of three commentaries. Rashi says that Abraham fully expected Lot to stay on the straight and narrow path – but that was not Lot's expectation. When Abraham suggests that they separate, Abraham is committing to rescue him (Rashi 13:9). Why would he do that for a person who is not righteous?

Lot saw the separation from Abraham in a different way. According to Rashi, when the Torah reports that Lot went east (13:11), it means that Lot distanced himself from God. When the Torah reports that the people of Sodom were evil, Rashi (13:13) explains that this verse is faulting Lot, for he did not hold back from living with evil people. Rashi (13:14) reveals that already when Lot was with Abraham, God had stopped talking to Abraham due to that association.

Radak takes a much more charitable view of Lot's actions. When Abraham tells Lot that the entire land is open for him (13:9), Radak interprets this to mean that Lot has merited the land through his worship of God. Radak explains that when Lot chose Sodom (13:11), his faith was so strong that he was confident he would not learn from Sodom's evil ways. Apparently, Lot was overconfident, since his level of observance was negatively affected in Sodom.

Another insight is provided by Chizkuni (13:12). When the Torah says that Lot went to Sodom, it actually says "moved his tent until Sodom." The word "until" indicates Lot's righteousness – he did not actually enter Sodom, due to its wickedness.

The commentators differ on when and why Lot went bad, and perhaps they differ in how bad he became. But one thing is clear. When Abraham and Lot initially split, at least in Abraham's eyes, Lot was still righteous.

It is interesting that even after the split, there are continued indications of Lot's worthiness. Abraham spends all of chapter 14 rescuing Lot. He spends the end of chapter 18 arguing with God to save Sodom on account of Lot's worthiness. He repeatedly refers to Lot as *tzaddik* (a righteous person), although it is not explicit in the text that "righteous" refers to Lot. Indeed, in chapter 19, God's messengers rescue Lot – he must have been worthy.

We can now explain why Abraham allowed Lot to go to Sodom and that it was not mistreatment on Abraham's part.

Abraham was on a mission. He was to transmit the word of God. The core leadership of this mission was Abraham and Sarah. Lot was the first lieutenant. A brother to Sarah, a nephew and brother-in-law to Abraham, he was a close family member. He voluntarily left the comforts of Charan to go on the mission. He faithfully followed Abraham to Canaan, to Egypt, and to the Negev.

A point came when they could not stay together, apparently based on economic reasons – their respective flocks had become too large. Abraham saw this as an opportunity. Abraham suggested separating. They could broaden the mission to multiple locations in the country. There would be no reason to avoid a sinful city like Sodom – the whole point of the mission was to confront evil and bring people to God. That had worked in Egypt. Why not attempt it in Sodom as well?

This explains Abraham's motivation for allowing Lot to go to Sodom in the first place and helps us appreciate his motivation for saving Lot in chapter 14. Lot was Abraham's assistant in his massive mission. If he was captured, Abraham was obligated to save him.

As it turned out, Lot's mission failed. He did not bring the Sodomites under the wings of God. Whether he never expected to (as Rashi seems to explain) or simply failed after trying (as Radak seems to imply), in the end it did not work out. But at least we can understand the motivations.

Deuteronomy validates Lot's worthiness. When the Jews approach the Land of Israel, God cautions them not to do battle with the two nations that are descendants of Lot – Moab (Deuteronomy 2:9) and Ammon (Deuteronomy 2:19). God says that He has deeded the land to these two nations.

This gesture to Lot is extraordinary. Consider the source. In Genesis 15:18–21, God deeds the land of ten nations to Abraham. Rashi (15:19) explains that the land of seven of these nations was provided to the Jewish people, two were provided to Lot, and one to Esau (whom we will deal with in chapters 7 and 8).

Compare the inheritance of Jacob (seven nations) to that of Lot (two nations). Certainly, Jacob received much more. But his descendants had to work so much harder to merit this inheritance. That included hundreds of years of slavery (15:13). It included a permanent obligation to fulfill the 613 mitzvot incumbent upon the Jews.

There must be something great and fundamental in Lot's contributions that he received the reward of the land of two nations. Rashi explains (Deuteronomy 2:5) that he received the reward because he did not reveal to Pharoah that Sarah was Abraham's wife. It is hard to imagine that single act of heroism deserved such merit – more likely, this single grant is the reward for a lifetime of good actions.

Although Lot received a huge reward (the land of two nations) for relatively little work, the reward was considerably less than the reward to the Jewish people. The commitment of Israel is everlasting (13:15). But in Numbers 21:26, we are taught that when Sichon displaced Moab from part of their land, that eliminated the commitment of that land to Moab. The commitment to Lot was not everlasting. That enabled the Jews to ultimately inherit the land, since they conquered it from Sichon – not from Moab (Rashi, ibid.). Further, Jewish women are instructed not to marry men from Ammon and Moab due to their anti-Jewish behavior as the Jews prepared to enter Israel (Deuteronomy 23:4, 5).

Despite these limitations, God's reward to Lot lasted nearly one thousand years. Based on a verse in Jeremiah (48:11), the Talmud (*Megillah* 12b) says that these two nations had quiet in their lands even longer than the Jews in Israel, lasting until the time of Esther and Mordechai (the main personages in the Book of Esther, which relates events that took place in Persia around 479 BCE). It seems that our Sages took the positive approach to valuing Lot's contributions.

In Jewish history, Lot is not obliterated. Through his descendant Ruth, Lot provides bloodlines to the Davidic dynastic and ultimately to the Messiah.

Treatment of Hagar and Ishmael

Hagar and Ishmael play outsized roles in the ten tests and in the life of Abraham. Three of the ten tests (numbers 5, 8, and 9) were related to that side of Abraham's family. We saw in chapter 2 that these tests involved belief (test 9), obedience (test 8), and commitment to transmission (test 5). We discussed how Abraham passed those tests, believing in Divine Providence, obeying His commands, and being steadfast in transmission.

In this chapter, we are trying to understand the righteousness of Abraham's behavior at the human level. Let's recount the stories and why they need explanation.

After Sarah suggests to Abraham that he take Hagar, who immediately becomes pregnant, Hagar loses respect for Sarah (16:4). Abraham does not facilitate the dispute between his long-term wife and the woman carrying his fetus – he simply tells Sarah to do what she pleases with Hagar (16:6). He does not seek kindness for Hagar. He does not arbitrate. Sarah's response is equally troubling – she oppresses Hagar (16:6), causing her to flee. At the encouragement of an angel, Hagar returns.

Later, after Isaac is born, Hagar's son Ishmael is fooling around with Isaac (21:9). The commentaries view this fooling around as quite serious – Rashi explains that it relates to idolatry, inappropriate sexual behavior, or murder. As a result, Sarah tells Abraham to throw Hagar and Ishmael out of the house (21:10). This troubles Abraham (21:11), yet God confirms that throwing Ishmael out is the right thing to do (21:12).

Let's examine these behaviors. On the one hand, it is not hard to argue that Sarah and Abraham were justified in forcing this exile. The crimes of which Ishmael was accused were severe. God Himself confirmed that banishment was the correct punishment.

On the other hand, while Abraham did not rush to judgment (21:11), he could have done something to rehabilitate Ishmael. This is the same Abraham who to defend the evil city of Sodom spent eleven verses (18:23–33) to forestall the destruction. Could he not have done more to protect or defend his own son? The fact that Ishmael repents later in life (Rashi 25:9) indicates that Ishmael was not a lost cause.

Indeed, the Talmud (*Baba Kamma* 93a) criticizes Sarah's behavior. If the Talmud found fault, who are we to exonerate Sarah entirely?

Could Ishmael Ever Have Been Chosen?

Let's assess whether it was ever possible for Ishmael to be part of the Chosen People. We start here not to denigrate Ishmael, but to recall the very high standards of Abraham and Sarah's home. This assessment is especially apt because of the great love that Abraham had for Ishmael, as described above in chapter 2. Abraham *wanted* Ishmael in the Chosen People

We understand what it means today for Jews to be the Chosen People. They have a covenant with God to observe a set of formal responsibilities above and beyond the seven Noahide laws. Further, children of a Jewish mother are automatically Jewish. The Chosen People is a set of individuals linked by covenant, commandments, and relationships. This is not an exclusively hereditary position; converts are free to join the Jewish people, and then their children are also part of the Chosen People.

The question of Ishmael's qualifications to be part of the Chosen People is a puzzle: Why was Abraham not able to pass the title of "chosen" to all his descendants? Why was his son Ishmael – prominent in distinction to the children of Keturah – not chosen? Said differently, what could or should Abraham have done to ensure that Ishmael was chosen? Abraham begot other children in Genesis 25. Why didn't Esau, the son of Isaac and Rebecca and the grandson of Abraham and Sarah, remain in the Chosen People? (See chapters 7 and 8 for this latter discussion.) This deepens the question of whether Abraham's actions were correct.

To explain this further, we repeat: the story of Genesis describes how the Chosen People are qualified by their demonstration of belief, obedience, and commitment to transmission. After Jacob, all relevant descendants are in the Chosen People whether or not they personally have the three qualifications. But God wanted the *initial* covenantal community limited to those who had the qualifications. While Abraham intuited that all his descendants *could* be part of this mission, God insisted on the qualifications.

Ishmael's behavior demonstrated that he was not qualified. Only Abraham's seed who themselves had the qualifications could proceed in the Chosen People. According to our Sages, Ishmael was not even fulfilling the seven Noahide laws, so he and his descendants were not qualified to be obligated in the 613 mitzvot.

Accordingly, Sarah, with her superior prophetic powers (Rashi 21:12), sees that it is impossible to achieve Abraham's dream of incorporating Ishmael into the covenantal family. She commands that Hagar and Ishmael be expelled (21:10), and God Himself confirms this decision (21:12). Why would God get in the middle of a domestic dispute if there were no cosmic importance? It must be that keeping Hagar and Ishmael was incompatible with the mission. Banishment, as hurtful as it was, was the appropriate behavior.

To be sure, this answer only works because of the distinction between the Chosen People and the *initial* Chosen People. The Torah is replete with descriptions of evil or imperfect Jewish people. They may be evil, but they are still Jewish. The Torah describes many misdeeds performed by Jews. Reuven makes mistakes (35:22), the brothers sell Joseph (37:28), Er does evil in the eyes of God (38:7), Korach incites a rebellion (Numbers chapter 16), and there are many other cases. They all remain Jews.

In the Prophets, there are even more examples of Jews gone astray. Some, like Jeroboam (I Kings 12:28), have no share in the World to Come (Mishnah, *Sanhedrin* 10:2) – but they are still Jews.

It is not even clear that it is fair to characterize Ishmael as totally evil. True, Ishmael is criticized as having a bad influence on Isaac (21:9). But in the end, he does repent (Rashi 25:9). Nonetheless, despite the fact that Ishmael had some redeeming characteristics, God decided that he did not qualify to be part of the first family of the covenant. Hence, irrespective of his redeeming characteristics, he needed to be banished.

Banishment Was Appropriate

While the previous section indicated that Ishmael could not remain because he did not have the positive attributes of the three qualifications, commentaries are harsher. They focus on the negative: Hagar and Ishmael's sins were so severe that they needed to be banished.

Let's begin with Genesis chapter 16. Initially, Sarah favored Hagar's advancement to be a co-wife (rather than a concubine; compare 25:6 and Ramban 16:3). Ramban infers from the end of the verse – "And Abraham hearkened to the voice of Sarah" – that Abraham *only* took Hagar at Sarah's direction. Hagar's entire status upgrade was due to Sarah. In 16:3, again, Abraham only took Hagar when Sarah physically gave her to Abraham.

In 16:4, when Hagar disrespected Sarah, our Sages do not see it as a small slight. Hagar had been a maidservant. Sarah went to great lengths to upgrade her status. True, Sarah had ulterior motives – to build her own family. But Sarah could have built the family in a different way, by selecting someone else for Abraham to take; she didn't have to elevate Hagar to be a co-wife. Although Sarah took every step to do well for Hagar, there was no reciprocity. Instead, Hagar despised Sarah.

Our Sages explained Hagar's disrespect as stemming from the most audacious root. Rashi (16:4, s.v. *"va'takal gevirtah b'eineha"*) suggests that Hagar asserted that Sarah was not really righteous, with the proof being that Sarah could not conceive for so many years, yet Hagar immediately became pregnant.

This created an untenable situation in the household. What to do? Sarah complains to Abraham. As Chizkuni explains, the complaint is reasonable.

Sarah showed great respect to both Hagar and Abraham and is only getting disrespect in return. Sarah says: "My wrong be upon you" (16:5). Chizkuni explains Sarah's anger. On the one hand, Abraham is not defending Sarah's honor. On the other hand, Sarah is reluctant to make Hagar suffer – after all, Hagar is now Abraham's wife. It is now an impossible situation. No one knows what to do. Abraham himself does not know what to do – Hagar is now his wife. Aren't there now limitations on what he can say to her? How does the household get repaired? Sarah asks God to make a judgment (16:5).

In such a tough situation, Abraham and Sarah could not demonstrate exemplary behavior because there was no perfect path. Abraham did not feel empowered to tell Hagar how she must behave. He could not fix the problem. All he could do was choose a side. In 16:6, Abraham simply says that Sarah can take control of the situation.

We can understand Sarah's behavior better if we link this vignette to Genesis chapter 21. Commentaries are very critical of Ishmael's behavior there. Sarah with her prophetic power could have foreseen very early that first Hagar, then Ishmael would negatively impact the ethics of the household. Her reaction is influenced by her prophetic insight of what would be Ishmael's future.

According to the text, Ishmael's crime was that he was "making sport" with Isaac (21:9). As we said above, Rashi explains that the term means idolatry, illicit sexual behavior, or murder. Rashi finds textual support for a variety of crimes.

Rashi gives an additional interpretation: Ishmael was taunting Isaac that as the elder, he would inherit a double portion of Abraham's estate. This is a less awful crime than the other three, but it speaks to the key mission of the life of Abraham.

Sforno has an interesting interpretation. He says that Ishmael was propagating a false rumor that Isaac was actually Abimelech's son. One could easily see how that would enrage Sarah. In response, Sarah lashes out (21:10). Her focus is on comparing Ishmael to Isaac. Sforno claims that Ishmael is an inappropriate heir as compared to Isaac for the following reasons:

• Ishmael is an idolator/immoral person/murderer.
• He has poor manners, as seen from his claim that he will get two portions.

- Since in the end, Hagar is undeserving of being a "wife," Ishmael's inheritance will come from Hagar – not Abraham.

Sarah was giving a human reaction to the insult of Ishmael's behavior. God does not deal with the minutiae of all of Sarah's grievances. God says simply that Abraham should listen to Sarah, because Isaac will get the covenantal mission (21:12). God Himself accepts Sarah's directions. Sarah understands instinctively that Isaac needs a well sheltered upbringing, away from distracting influences.

What can we say about the appropriateness of Abraham's response? After Sarah begs Abraham to expel Hagar and Ishmael, Abraham is conflicted (21:11). He does not want to expel them. Two things change his mind. In 21:12, God commands him to do so, and Abraham is obedient. That's what test 8 is all about. But God also senses that He must mollify Abraham. In 21:13, God assures Abraham that Ishmael, too, will be great. As Radak explains, Abraham has a legitimate concern about negative consequences to Ishmael resulting from the expulsion. Only once Abraham's legitimate concerns are addressed can Abraham move on to accept that the mission of transmission will only be through Isaac. With this, Abraham safely passes test 9. He need not worry about being too harsh, because God has guaranteed that a positive fate is sealed for Ishmael.

How could Abraham have expelled Hagar and Ishmael with so few provisions (21:14)? The expulsion occurs after God tells him that Ishmael will become a nation. Divine Providence will watch over Ishmael – Abraham's responsibilities are done.

It is important to recognize that Ishmael is not actually rejected. He will become a great nation. He will later repent and join Isaac in burying Abraham (25:9). But although he is not rejected, he is not at the level to join the covenant.

Once God communicated that the inheritance of Abraham only goes to Isaac, it is clear why Abraham sent away the sons of Keturah, a later wife whom he married after Sarah (25:6; some say that Keturah is actually Hagar, whom he remarried). Ramban (25:6) says that Abraham learned that *only* Isaac would inherit the mission from this same verse above (21:12).

Sarah, Abraham, and Abimelech

Let's turn to the second visit to foreign lands. In chapter 20, Abraham visits the land of Gerar, and again Sarah is represented as his sister. King Abimelech takes her, but God warns Abimelech, causing Sarah to be returned. There is one additional troubling verse.

Abraham tells Abimelech that representing his wife as his sister was not a spur-of-the-moment, unplanned trick. He says that when he began wandering, he told Sarah that "at *every* place whither we shall come, say of me: he is my brother" (20:13). It was preplanned. Although some (see Radak, s.v. "*el kol makom*") interpret "every" to mean only these two times, we see that this was going to potentially be a regular lie – and we know it happened at least twice.

Hence this vignette provokes the same questions as the Pharoah vignette, although with a greater intensity due to the repetition. Of course, the answers may be the same. Either Abraham's behavior was appropriate due to the priority of saving lives, or perhaps he divorced Sarah first, so there was nothing formally wrong.

One interesting question about test 7 is to understand why Gerar is considered an independent test. Abraham and Sarah had already been tested in this situation. Namely, if a monarch takes Sarah, potentially ruining the plan of transmission that Abraham and Sarah had diligently laid out, would they continue undaunted in their mission? We already know the answer – they passed the Pharoah test. What is new about test 7?

One new element is the change in the family situation. Abraham and Sarah had always assumed that they were partners in the mission of transmission. From 12:7 onward, Abraham knew that he would have offspring who would inherit the land. But as the years went by, they might have begun to wonder whether Abraham would have offspring through Sarah. After all, God had not originally promised that there would be offspring through Sarah. Despair set in. Sarah gave her maidservant to Abraham so that she could be built from her – but thirteen years had passed since that event, and still they had no child. Even worse, perhaps, with Ishmael, Abraham already had an heir.

God appeared to Abraham (17:19), and the angels visited Abraham and Sarah (18:10). Finally, at ages ninety-nine and eighty-nine respectively, they were told that God guaranteed they would have a son, Isaac. At long last, their dream would be fulfilled.

This created a different psychology as they approached Abimelech. They might have had low expectations when they appeared before Pharoah. Abraham had been promised offspring, and so the situation with Pharoah was a mild challenge, but perhaps the offspring would come from a different wife, and he was not destined to stay with Sarah.

By the time they approached Abimelech, much had changed. On the positive side, God's commitment that Abraham's mission of fathering a Chosen People was now extended to be a commitment to create the Chosen People with Sarah. Their joy was unbridled. Their expectation could not be contained. Everything they had lived for would happen. Would God maintain this commitment to them?

As a result, when again confronted with the possibility that Sarah would be taken from Abraham, could they withstand this test again? Also, Ishmael was on the scene. Was Sarah being taken by Abimelech a prologue to moving the covenant to Ishmael? From many perspectives, believing in the commitment was becoming difficult.

Thus, it was a crashing blow when they found themselves in the same impossible situation that they had been in with Pharaoh. This was a new test – to see if Abraham and Sarah could maintain their faith and their commitment to the mission of transmission despite being taken from the highest possible high to a crashing low. Could Sarah maintain her dedication knowing that Ishmael was on the scene, waiting in the wings? Yet they succeeded and passed this test as well.

The Binding of Isaac

Unquestionably, the most strenuous test for Abraham was the binding of Isaac. God tests Abraham's faith by asking him to bind Isaac and sacrifice him on an altar. Abraham responds with blind faith, and the text of Genesis chapter 22 lauds him for doing so. It was such a clear test that – as opposed to the other nine tests – it was actually called a "test" in the Torah (22:1). In chapter 2, we pointed out that this tested all of Abraham's qualifying characteristics simultaneously: obedience, belief, and his mission of transmission. Abraham *obeyed* and *maintained his belief* despite the fact that obeying seemed to be contrary to his belief system. God's asking Abraham to sacrifice his son would have caused an ordinary man to wonder whether the mission of transmission was viable, but Abraham was not dissuaded.

There is no question that God devised a devious test to demonstrate Abraham's worthiness. And there is no question that Abraham in fact demonstrated his worthiness. Despite God previously promising that Abraham's legacy would come through Isaac (21:12), Abraham had faith in God and plunged ahead to do the action that would apparently render God's promise null and void.

We need to understand the underlying ethics. Blind faith in the Creator, such as Abraham exhibited in leaving his home to go to Canaan (Genesis chapter 12), is one thing and laudable. If the only issue with the binding of Isaac is the apparent undercutting of God's promise to Abraham, it would still be hard to understand – but perhaps not impossible. Maybe Abraham had misunderstood God's promise. Maybe it was consistent for God to promise a legacy through Isaac, but then ask Abraham to apparently uproot that promise.

But the problem here was more basic. Abraham was being asked to kill his son, a frank violation of the Noahide laws (9:5–6). God was not simply asking him to take an action that was difficult. He was asking him to violate His own prohibitions.

Under those circumstances, it is not clear that the right way to pass the test is to follow God's command. Could Abraham have demonstrated worthiness without almost taking Isaac to be slaughtered? Why not take a different course of action? Why not question God as he did at Sodom (18:23)?

Following Rashi's explanation (22:5, s.v. "*v'nashuvah*"), Abraham intuited that God was not asking him to slaughter Isaac. Abraham understood God to be setting up a situation with a dual interpretation. A naïve interpretation of the command was that Abraham was being asked to slaughter Isaac. But Abraham simply chose, at every step of the way, to give God the benefit of the doubt, as it were. That is, he assumed that although God was implying that he would need to slaughter Isaac, He didn't intend for Abraham to do so in the end. There would be some other explanation for God's words. To some extent, that was part of his extraordinary belief.

With that duality, Abraham had no difficulty being obedient. His willingness to follow instructions punctuated his belief that in the end things would work out. He knew that he would never truly jeopardize the path of transmission by taking Isaac's life.

This begins with the start of God's commandment. In 22:2, God commands Abraham to perform this test. The language that God uses is "*Lech lecha*," which literally means that Abraham should "go," but interestingly is exactly the same phrase that God uses when he initiates Abraham into the godly mission in 12:1. God is signaling that this new strange request is all *part of* the primary mission of Abraham's life.

In 22:2, God continues with "offer him there for a burnt offering." But the word "offer" has a dual meaning in Hebrew. Rashi interprets the word to mean "lift" him. Rashi explains that God didn't say that Abraham should sacrifice Isaac. By using a word that could mean "lift," God was implying that Abraham would perform a symbolic lifting, but not go forward with the murderous deed. Rashi repeats this in 22:12 (s.v. "*ki atah*").

As Abraham continues on his journey, on the third day, Abraham tells the two accompanying lads that they need go no further. Abraham and Isaac will continue on the journey alone. Abraham says: "We will worship and come back to you" (22:5). Rashi says that Abraham prophesied that they were both coming back. In other words, he was following God's commandment, but he knew that no evil would befall Isaac.

We need to scrutinize all of Abraham's actions. In 22:6, Abraham takes a knife and fire. If his only intention was to do a symbolic lifting of Isaac, why did he need a knife and fire?

It seems clear from the continuation of the narrative that part of how Abraham would fulfill God's wish was to actually sacrifice something. In 22:13, Abraham locates a ram and sacrifices it. Whereas much of Genesis chapter 22 demonstrates Abraham following the direction of God (taking his son, going to Mount Moriah, preparing the altar), this action to locate and sacrifice a ram was not commanded by God. Abraham planned it all along, including the bringing of the knife and the fire. After all, in 22:2, God said there would be a burnt offering. Verse 22:13 is explicit. The ram is not a random offering. It was brought "in the stead of his son."

Also supporting the theory that Abraham never expected to actually kill his son is Rashi's interpretation of verse 22:6, "they went both of them together." They had a unity of purpose. Rashi explains that although Abraham understood that the literal mission was to slaughter Isaac, he was as joyous as Isaac, who did not hear God's commandment. How is it possible that Abraham was actually joyous about the upcoming murder, if not for the recognition that there was going to be another way to explain God's strange request?

The duality in God's commandment is best expressed in 22:8. Isaac had asked why they were not traveling with a sacrificial lamb (22:7). Abraham answered, "God will provide Himself the lamb for a burnt offering, my son." Rashi interprets the verse to express the duality. Abraham is confident that God will provide a sacrificial lamb. But if He doesn't, then "my son." In other words, Isaac might be the sacrifice himself. Abraham is both expressing his belief that this is only a test (there will be a lamb), but also his willingness to go through all the motions to follow the literal commandment of God.

The dramatic climax of the story occurs in 22:9–10. Abraham builds the altar, arranges the wood, binds Isaac, and reaches out to take the knife to slaughter his son. Most of the actions are consistent with either of the dual notions – to "lift" Isaac on the altar or to "slaughter" Isaac on the altar. But what about the last action – taking the knife to slaughter his son?

Many of the commentators (e.g., Rashi) are remarkably silent on this verse. What was going through Abraham's mind? What were his true intentions? Let's say hypothetically that the angel had not come along (22:11) to tell Abraham not to harm Isaac. What would Abraham have done? Would he have gone through with the slaughter? That is the key question of the ethics of the binding.

Assuredly, Abraham was knowledgeable in the seven Noahide laws. He knew that he was not permitted to take anyone's life – certainly not his son's. The angel was not telling him anything new when he said, "Lay not your hand upon the lad" (22:12). There is no way that Abraham would have slaughtered Isaac.

If that's the case, then what was the test? The test was to see how far Abraham would go. God was testing his obedience. Would he be obedient up to the ultimate point where the next action would contravene God's own law? Does this affect his belief in God's faithfulness? Will this dissuade him from his mission? The test was never whether he would carry out murder per se. As Rashi explained, Abraham knew that from the outset. But to pass the test, he needed to participate in the charade yet nonetheless continue his total dedication to the life mission.

Abraham does not need the angel to tell him to stop. He grabs the knife. He would have stayed there forever, but he would not have done the final action. The angel could just as easily be his inner voice telling him *No, a Noahide cannot murder.*

The angel has a different role. It is to tell Abraham, "neither do you anything to him" (22:12), which Rashi interprets to mean that Abraham should not even cause Isaac a small blemish. Perhaps if there were no way out, Abraham would have addressed God's request with symbolic bloodletting. That was already done at Isaac's circumcision – perhaps this is a replay. The angel stops even that. And the angel finishes by telling Abraham of his merit (22:16–18).

The Search for Isaac's Wife
Chapter 24 describes Abraham's dispatching of Eliezer to find a wife for Isaac from Aram, rather than from Canaan. Viewed through modern egalitarian sensibilities, one wonders whether choosing a mate based on ethnic, national considerations is acceptable. Of course, the mate needed to be the right person for Isaac – but why decide a priori which nationality the person should come from? Especially since Abraham and Sarah brought many local Canaanites to see the ways of the true God.

This issue is deepened by Rabbi Samson Raphael Hirsch. He points out (24:4) that the Arameans were also idolators. What was the benefit of going to Aram?

He provides two insights. First, Hirsch hypothesizes that aside from the common sin of idolatry, there was a more general moral degeneracy in Canaan. Isaac's wife needed to be free of that.

More significantly, from the word *b'kirbo* ("among whom I dwell," 24:4), he infers that the real problem with Canaanites (compared to Arameans) is not that Canaanites were inherently worse. Since Isaac lived in Canaan, any Canaanite wife would always be close to the influences of her family. An

Aramean wife could be pulled away from the idolatrous family influences once brought to Canaan.

Kli Yakar (24:3) adds an additional point. Keeping the wife apart from her birth family was the reason that Abraham commanded Eliezer, "Beware that you bring not my son back there" (24:6). If Isaac had gone to Aram, then marrying Aramean women there would be no better than marrying a Canaanite woman in Canaan. The key was to bring the wife away from her home influences to Isaac in Canaan.

It is interesting that Abraham intuited in 24:6 that Isaac should not leave Canaan. Later (26:2), when Isaac planned to go to Egypt during a famine, God *commanded* Isaac not to leave Canaan. Rashi explains that Isaac had the status of a holy burnt offering – presumably due to his binding at the altar; hence he could not leave the Holy Land. But Abraham apparently reached the same conclusion for different reasons in Genesis chapter 24.

In appendix 1, we catalogue thirty vignettes in Abraham's life and identify that at least eight of them seem to reflect poorly on Abraham in some respects. We have now completed an explanation of these vignettes. God placed Abraham in difficult situations that had no easy solution. Abraham satisfied the tests by remaining committed to obedience, belief, and transmission. While superficially, Abraham may have appeared to respond to some of the tests with questionable ethics, one sees upon closer inspection that he behaved properly. For a summary chart, see appendix 3.

Chapter 6

Abraham among the Canaanites

We have completed the central analysis of chapters 12–25 in Genesis, which discuss the life story of Abraham. Threaded through this narrative are sub-themes that enrich our understanding of Abraham's journey. Chapter 6 will review Abraham's encounter with the Canaanites. We will especially explain the relevance of the long story of Sodom and Gomorrah.

Living among the Canaanite Nations

Abraham's mission was not to create an *insular* Chosen People, but to model godliness to all nations of the world. Evidently, to achieve that, the Jewish people would need to be in constant contact with other nations. For Abraham to qualify for this mission, he would need to demonstrate facility in dealing with the challenges of living a life surrounded by immoral people. In the biblical narrative, the Canaanites are portrayed as the most immoral of all. They play a special role in the selection of Abraham as progenitor of the Chosen People.

According to Genesis, it is the children of Cham who are most responsible for the dispersion. Their attack on morality occurs immediately after the deluge. Noah's son Cham, in conjunction with his son Canaan, attacks the drunken Noah, and the two of them are cursed (9:22–27). Canaan's nephew (also from Cham) is the Nimrod who is responsible for the Tower of Babel (Rashi 10:8) and for throwing Abraham into the fiery furnace (Rashi 11:28). The Canaanites and their close relatives play a key role as the target audience for Abraham's mission. Abraham has to live with them and needs to influence them. He has superlative success, as seen in the trusted relationship with Eliezer, grandson of Nimrod. Hence Canaanites appear throughout this section of the Torah.

Other Canaanite tribes that Abraham will encounter are Canaan's son Heth (10:15 and 23:3), the Amorites (10:16 and 15:16), Sodom and Gomorroh

(10:19 and chapters 14 and 19), and the Philistines (10:14 and chapters 20 and 21).

These constant references to the Canaanites emphasize Abraham's mission. He demonstrates the ethical plane required by God. This informs these nations of the requirement to follow God's laws – the seven Noahide laws. These nations do not get the message. When the Jews return from exile in Egypt, God disinherits them from the Land of Israel.

Looking at Genesis sequentially, the references start at the very beginning. When Abraham first comes to Canaan, the Torah emphasizes, "the Canaanite was then in the land" (12:6). Other references to the descendants of Cham include:

- the visit to Egypt (12:6–20)
- the Canaanites and Perizi in the land (13:7)
- Lot's travel to Sodom (13:10–13)
- the nine kings, many of them from Cham (chapter 14)
- God's promise of Canaanite lands to Abraham (15:16–21)
- Ishmael's Egyptian mother (16:3)
- the destruction of Sodom (chapters 18, 19)
- interactions with Abimelech the king of the Philistines (chapters 20 and 21)
- negotiating Sarah's burial with the people of Heth (chapter 23)
- the idea that Isaac should not marry a Canaanite (24:3)

These references are indicative that the mission of the Jews, as a light upon all nations, is to confront sinfulness directly and show the way of God.

The Land of Israel and the Canaanites

Another subtheme of these chapters is the importance of the Land of Israel, evidenced in the many promises God makes to Abraham about the Land. We find this theme in 12:7, 13:14–15, 15:18–21, and 17:8. The Land of Israel is invested by God with special sanctity, and its bequeathal to Abraham is an important part of his blessings. God wants the Chosen People in the Chosen Land.

Abraham might have been uncomfortable with the idea of displacing the existing inhabitants of the land; his commitment was to try to bring all people to the path of God. He was the supreme transmitter. He was involved in converting people in Charan. He embraced everyone, including his son Ishmael and his right-hand man, Eliezer. This caused a tension between Abraham's being selected to inherit Canaan and his attempts to redeem the people living there, challenging God's plan to remove them from the Land of Israel.

God had apparently given up on the Canaanites. He foresaw that there was no redeeming them. God was comfortable entering into a binding covenant with Abraham to deed Israel to the Chosen People. In the same measure that Abraham's outreach toward the sinners was threaded throughout the biblical text, God's understanding of the futility of this was woven as well. Irrespective of Abraham's optimism, Omniscient God knew better. Omniscient God could even pinpoint how long it would take to cement the complete degradation of the sons of Cham. He told Abraham that it would take four hundred years (15:13), because the iniquity of the Amorites would not be full until the fourth generation (15:16).

Nowhere was the contrast between Abraham's embrace of Canaanites and the futility of that enterprise more apparent than in the story of Sodom and Gomorrah. The larger story of Sodom and Gomorrah (chapters 18 and 19) is covered in the next section, but there are hints of this even earlier.

Chapter 14 is the battle of the nine kings during which Abraham actually saves Sodom, in addition to several other nations. It is interesting to see how the Torah reports on the result of the victory. Abraham is approached by two contemporary kings: Malkizedek (14:18–20) and the king of Sodom (14:17 and 14:21–24). The reactions of these two kings could not be more different.

In the case of Malkizedek, the emphasis is on blessing God and blessing Abraham in the name of God. The Sages associate Malkizedek with Shem the son of Noah. In other words, Malkizedek is the original Semite.

The king of Sodom, by contrast, emphasizes dividing the loot. He insists that he needs to be the recipient of those who were captured. That itself is rather aggressive – he had been captured and Abraham saved him. Why does he deserve anything? And when Abraham disclaims any benefit, leaving it all to the king of Sodom, there is nary a protest word coming from the Sodomite.

Even Ephron, when selling a burial plot for Sarah, initially expresses a willingness to provide the plot gratis (23:11).

After that display of gross thanklessness in Genesis chapter 14, it is not surprising that God is comfortable with Abraham being promised Canaan in chapter 15.

Genesis also illustrates that the Canaanite kings were aware of Abraham's ascendancy and his ultimate role to displace them. But this is done in very subtle ways:

- While Abraham saves five kings in the battle of the nine kings (chapter 14), the respite for these five Canaanite kings is temporary. Four of the five are wiped out in chapter 19 with the destruction of Sodom and Gomorrah (see Deuteronomy 29:22). Only the fifth, Tsoar, seems to survive (see 19:22).
- In the first encounter with Abimelech the king of the Philistines, after Abimelech sees God's hand, he tells Abraham to live wherever he pleases (20:15).
- In the second encounter with Abimelech, after Abimelech sees that the heir (Isaac) is born, Abimelech tries to establish a long-term relationship with the ascendant Abraham (21:23).
- Ephron and the people of Heth express a willingness to give over burial ground to Abraham, gratis (23:6 and 23:11).

It is possible that there was insincerity involved in some of these encounters, but we do see the Canaanite leaders trying to awkwardly find some accommodation with this new movement of Abraham.

Sodom and Gomorrah's Broader Import

The story of Sodom and Gomorrah, covering the end of Genesis chapter 18 and all of chapter 19, bears no relationship to the genealogy of the Chosen People and is not part of the ten tests. Why does this story belong in the holy Torah at all?

To be sure, there are important messages in this story. It shows reward and punishment on a large scale, as God continues to deal with evil in postdiluvian times. In chapter 1, we explained that God introduced the story (and the dialog with Abraham) to exemplify the concepts of belief and obedience that Abraham needed to transmit. It also teaches us the genealogy of our cousins Ammon and Moab.

But despite these valuable pieces, it is still hard to justify relating such a long story just to reach those conclusions. The Torah's path is to be concise in its stories, without belaboring details.

Here are some questions:

- Why was it important for God to tell Abraham about the impending doom?
- What is the point of the long, unsuccessful bargaining between Abraham and God in 18:24–33?
- What was the cosmic importance of the destruction of Sodom that it took most of chapter 19 to describe? It seems unrelated to the main thread of Genesis.
- What is the symbolism implied by Lot's wife turning into a pillar of salt?

To address these questions, we will now retell the story of Sodom and Gomorrah – not as a story exclusively about the evil of the city, but more generally as part of the justification for deeding the Holy Land to the Jewish people rather than the original inhabitants.

Our first question above was why God told Abraham about the impending doom.

Let's elaborate on the question. Omniscient God sits in judgment of all souls. There is no record of Him checking in with Abraham when He makes decisions. Why does He ask, "Shall I hide from Abraham that which I am doing?" (18:17). Why is He asking the question? Why does Abraham need to know? What is special about this decision? This does not relate to Abraham's mission. Rashi and Rashbam say that God feels the obligation because it is part of Abraham's land. But that is weak – God had already told Abraham that ultimately the land would belong to his descendants.

From the context of Abraham's central mission, we know he was also motivated to proselytize the residents of Canaan. He was intending to bring them all on a godly path. He had dispatched Lot to convert the Sodomites. Lot was making progress. He endeared himself to them and had just been appointed

as a judge (Rashi 19:1, s.v. *"b'shaar Sedom"*). He was poised to begin the proselytizing process.

But God knew that it was not to be. Lot had been there for twenty-four
years with little success. Rather than raising the standards in Sodom, Lot was
being brought down by the Sodomites. God was ready to destroy Sodom. But
since Abraham had a different strategy for Sodom, it was only fair for God
to tell Abraham his plan. He could not simply break Abraham's mission of
outreach to all without an explanation. That was the imperative to introduce
the topic. God introduced the topic not to get Abraham's permission, but to
help Abraham understand the limitations of his mission.

That is why the Abraham-God dialog continues with 18:19 ("For I have
known him…that he may command his children…that they may keep the
way of the Lord…"). That verse describes the qualification of commitment to
transmission that we derived in chapter 1. The narrative is a perfect fit. God
recalls that one of Abraham's three key qualifications is commitment to transmission. Abraham is a master of outreach. But Abraham is wrong to assume
that his outreach will succeed with the entire world. As 18:19 says, God is
narrowing the application of the attribute of commitment to transmission.
The verse continues with "he may command his children and his household."
The Torah is telling us that while the universal outreach of Abraham may be
valuable, some of the unique transmission is limited to the Chosen People.

In the next verses, God continues to explain that Sodom and Gomorrah
are evil (18:20–21). They cannot be redeemed. They must be destroyed.

God is both narrowing the focus on Abraham's transmission specifically to
descendants and also clarifying the messages of the transmission. God wants
Abraham to transmit His messages to everyone. That's Abraham's job. But
God's job is to apply reward and punishment to all. God is communicating
that these two jobs can come into conflict – there might be situations when
God will decide to punish and eliminate sinners, and Abraham will therefore
not be able to transmit to them.

This explains the long back-and-forth between Abraham and God in
18:23–33 about how many righteous people are in Sodom. Superficially, one
wonders why either party is engaged in the dialog. Why does God care about
Abraham's point of view? Why is Abraham negotiating on behalf of sinful
cities? Doesn't Abraham trust God to do the right thing?

Viewed through the lens of outreach from Abraham and Lot to Sodom, the exchange fits better. God has come to Abraham to inform him that Sodom is irredeemable. Abraham is shattered. After all, he is trying to redeem the world. Lot has just been appointed as a judge in Sodom – a hopeful sign. But when Abraham learns the decree and hears that God will personally investigate (18:21), he bargains for criteria that might spare the city. It is not a random discussion. Abraham is investing in making his outreach city successful. God plays along. He allows Abraham to verbalize his hopes for outreach. That is the best God can offer. Unfortunately for Abraham, it is hopeless. In the end, there are fewer than ten righteous people in the city, and Sodom does not merit to be spared.

There is an ironic allusion in the middle of this negotiation. As Abraham presses the issue with God, he characterizes himself as "but dust and ashes" (18:27). Superficially, he is saying the obvious – that man has no standing before God.

Rashi views this as an allusion that he should have been dust (i.e., killed) in his fight with the kings and ashes (i.e., burnt) from his encounter with Nimrod in the furnace. Why does Rashi introduce the vignettes of the kings and the furnace here? These allusions have great resonance when one realizes that these were two notable instances in which God saved Abraham from the sons of Cham. It is as if Abraham is saying to God that he knows the evil of the sons of Cham; he has experienced it personally. He knows that God saved him – and he still wants to argue that these same sons of Cham can be redeemed. His experiences give him some standing to make that case.

If the simple message were that Sodom was evil, there could have been a more succinct description of the destruction. But that is not the purpose. The purpose is to show the larger tale of the irredeemability of the sons of Cham. To achieve that requires a demonstration of how low the morals had sunk at Sodom and how vile was the influence of the Sodomites. Lot, the nephew of Abraham, was at a higher level than them, but he was degraded by the association. This teaching – evident in the text itself – is emphasized further in the commentaries.

Here is how Rashi tells the story. Lot was becoming important, and he welcomed the angels (19:1) – something he had learned to do from Abraham. But Lot told them not to wash up, or it would look like they were long-term lodgers – anathema to the Sodomites. Nonetheless, the evil Sodomites heard about the guests, surrounded Lot's house, and said they wanted to sodomize the visitors (19:4–5). To push them off, Lot offered his virgin daughters instead – not exactly an act of high morals. Even that offer was not good enough, and the Sodomites rushed the door. The Midrash elaborates with further examples of evil. *Bereishit Rabbah* (51:5) says that Lot's wife later turned into a pillar of salt because she sinned with salt. She ran to all of her neighbors asking for salt for her guests, which is how they knew that Lot had guests.

The purpose of the detail is to show the total depravity of the Canaanites. In other words, to justify their displacement in favor of the Chosen People.

There are other oddities in the story that support the theory that the Sodom narrative does not stand alone but is tied in with the broader Genesis narrative.

In 19:20, Lot's wife looks at the destruction and becomes a pillar of salt. Above, we brought Rashi's explanation that she was punished with salt because she sinned with salt. Elsewhere in the Torah, salt refers to permanence. In Numbers 18:19, God describes His commitments to Aaron and the priests as an eternal covenant of salt. In this respect, Lot's wife turning to a pillar of salt can be viewed as God putting down a permanent marker. The Land of Israel must go to the holy Chosen People, not to the sinful. Even today in modern Israel, one can see a salt formation at the Dead Sea that is designated as Lot's wife. It is God's message that the Land of Israel is for the Chosen People.

One more curiosity. In the middle of the destruction, 19:27 says that Abraham got up early in the morning. The Talmud (*Berachot* 26b) says that Abraham was instituting the daily morning prayer (Radak 19:27). Superficially, this is bizarre. Why is prayer introduced in the middle of the destruction of some city that Abraham did not even live in? Why not when God first appeared to him (12:1) or when Isaac was born? Why here? Why was Abraham even relevant to the Sodom story?

In the context of our analysis, it is very logical. Abraham was brought into the Sodom story because God needed to show him that despite his efforts in outreach, the key covenant of the Chosen People would be with Isaac. Isaac alone would inherit the Land of Israel. Isaac was about to be born, and Abraham needed to accept that he was the unique heir. This is the same

Abraham who earlier that year (had exclaimed, "Oh, that Ishmael might live before You!" 17:18).

The Sodom story begins with God revealing His plans. Abraham unsuccessfully tries to find a reason for mercy. God proceeds with the destruction. At that point, Abraham must acknowledge that God was right and accept that the Chosen People line will go through Isaac. He acknowledges the point by inventing daily prayer. From now on, the Chosen People will thank God and accept our subservience on a daily basis.

The end of 19:27 emphasizes the connection. The place where he went to pray was the exact place in which a day earlier he had stood in front of God to negotiate the potential survival of Sodom. The symbolism is that he came full circle. Abraham could not find favor for Sodom, so he came back to God in prayer and prepared the path for the birth of the chosen son, Isaac.

Chapter 7

The Second Generation – Isaac and Rebecca

We now discuss the next generation, focusing on Isaac and his wife Rebecca.

Given that the central part of the Genesis narrative has been to identify and test the qualifications of the progenitor of the Chosen People, the first question is whether Isaac also needed to be tested. Did Abraham's successful tests clear the way for the Chosen People, or were there additional tests required for Isaac to be chosen as well? We don't have a tradition that Isaac had ten tests like Abraham. But is there some other element of testing in this portion of the Torah? Did Isaac need to be tested at all? Was his ascension to the patriarchy automatic at birth? After all, God had promised Abraham that the mantle would be passed through Isaac (17:19).

Certain incidents involving Isaac that resemble tests were apparently not tests. In 26:7, Isaac visits Gerar. Fearful that he will be killed on account of his wife, he follows Abraham's custom of announcing that Rebecca is his sister. He is unconcerned that they will take Rebecca as a wife for one of the locals. Superficially, this looks like a replay of tests 3 and 7 endured by Abraham. Is this a test whether he will lose confidence in the mission of transmission?

But deeper inspection reveals that this is not a test at all. First, Rebecca was in no real danger – this was a danger that Isaac imagined. Many commentaries point out that the reason Isaac did not fear being intimate with Rebecca in 26:8 was that after the declaration that she was his sister, no one went to take her. There was no real test.

Moreover, let's look at the contrast in timing. Sarah was taken by Pharoah and Abimelech before the birth of Isaac. Tests 3 and 7 challenged Abraham with the possibility that if Sarah were taken, there would be no heir from Abraham and Sarah to whom the Torah could be transmitted. But in the case of Isaac and Rebecca, Jacob had already been born. As we will soon see, the Torah had already been transmitted to Jacob. So even had Rebecca been taken, it would not have challenged the mission of transmission directly.

Another question is whether the Torah demonstrates Isaac's worthiness. Even if there were no formal test, perhaps the purpose of the Isaac story is to describe his worthiness in some other way.

We also have the recurring question: What is the purpose of the biblical text? The message that after Abraham was selected, he passed the mantle to Isaac and then Jacob could have been expressed very succinctly, in a few sentences. For the Torah to expand on this over several chapters means there is a broader message – and one that we must explore and understand.

How Esau Muddles the Status of Isaac

In the introduction, we discussed that what made Abraham different from Shem and Ever – prior great scholars and followers of God's path – was his dedication to the transmission of God's word to future generations. As a result, the Chosen People started with Abraham, not with his ancestors Shem and Ever. Those ancestors had offspring who went astray – but from Abraham onward, we had the Chosen People.

But, wait a minute! Esau was a direct descendant of Abraham and a child of Isaac and Rebecca. We learned in chapter 2 that God wanted the Chosen People to come from Sarah. That was why the mission went to Isaac and could not go to Ishmael or Abraham's other children. But once it went to Isaac, why wasn't Esau automatically included? It appears that Abraham is no different from Shem and Ever – some of his descendants are included in the Chosen People, but not all of them. This would seem to imply that Isaac was somehow not automatically in the Chosen People with his descendants. So there must have been some further qualification procedure.

Esau is a singularity. Starting with Jacob, all descendants are included in the Jewish people and God's covenant with Abraham. Some of Jacob's sons sinned, but they were not shunned. Compare with Esau, a son of Isaac and Rebecca who is excluded from the blessing of Abraham.

Breaking the question down, if Isaac were *automatically* included in the Chosen People by dint of his birthright, why not his son Esau? If Isaac were *not* included automatically, what qualifier did he pass to deserve the role of becoming the second Patriarch? And then we will need to understand the basis upon which Jacob also became a Patriarch and Esau did not.

In chapter 2, we discussed Abraham's expectation that Ishmael would share in the mission. Ishmael too was his son. Finally, God told him it would not be that way (17:20–21). Abraham did not accept this easily. He wanted the whole world to be part of this mission. Certainly, his son.

How much more should Isaac have felt that Esau needed to be part of the Chosen People, given that Esau was also the son of the chosen Matriarch, Rebecca?

Isaac's relationship with Esau is fascinating. At the beginning of Esau's life, he is Isaac's favored son (25:28). Later in life, when it is time to bless his sons, Isaac intends the primary blessing to go to his elder son Esau (27:4). How is this consistent with the role of the Patriarch to transmit God's message? Why bless the evil son? In chapter 27, Jacob disguises himself as Esau and extracts for himself the blessing that Isaac had intended for Esau. It is revealing what Isaac had intended for Esau.

First, Isaac provides an economic blessing – one that would be fitting for any and all of his sons: "God give you of the dew of the heaven, and of the fat places of the earth, and plenty of corn and wine" (27:28). Very nice, but unremarkable.

He continues that he intended much more for Esau. He starts with political leadership: "Let peoples serve you and nations bow down to you" (27:29). But remarkably, he even projects that Esau will dominate Jacob: "Be lord over your brethren and let your mother's sons bow down to you" (ibid.). This is not a blessing that he can give equally to any and all children – he is showing favoritism for Esau. He closes with "Cursed be everyone who curses you, and blessed be everyone who blesses you" (ibid.), echoing the very first blessing that Abraham got from God (12:3).

On the other hand, when Rebecca is pregnant with Esau and Jacob, God foreshadows that there will be no peace between Esau and Jacob. Rebecca plays a major role in the deceit that will result in Jacob getting the blessings (27:6–16). She also orchestrates Jacob's escape to avoid the retribution from Esau (27:42–46). Can we conclude from her interactions and actions that Esau's fate as the evil, non-inheriting son was determined at birth? Is there justice to that?

The centrality of Esau in these chapters implies that it must be a key purpose of chapters 25–28 to explain the logic of Isaac's love for Esau, why Esau is favored, why he is the target of blessings, and how this is consistent with God's ethical universe. Simultaneously, we have seen in chapters 12–25 that a purpose of Genesis is to teach us about the establishment of the Patriarchs and Matriarchs. What are the criteria and credentials? In this case, why is Jacob "in" and Esau "out"? Is it simply because Jacob was good and Esau was a sinner? But then, some of Jacob's sons also sinned. Why weren't they cast out?

Sealing the Decision about the Patriarchs

The previous section left us in a quandary. On the one hand, Abraham completed all the tests, and God rewarded him with blessings, commitments, and covenants. That might have implied that all his descendants were now part of the covenant. On the other hand, we know that Esau was excluded from these covenants. It seems that the qualification procedure was not yet complete.

Our Sages try to address this quandary by looking at 21:12. God tells Abraham that "*in* Isaac will be your seed." They infer that Abraham's legacy will be "*in* Isaac," but not "all of Isaac." Notably, Esau does not get Abraham's legacy.

This derivation illustrates our Sages' discomfort with the fact that Esau is excluded. They needed a biblical verse to explain why it happened. Unfortunately, this verse does not provide a very good answer. It does explain the *fact* that Esau is excluded. But it does not describe the *mechanism* or the *rationale*.

To address the quandary that Esau was excluded from the covenant but Jacob's sinning descendants were included leads to the inescapable conclusion that the testing procedure was not yet complete; more needed to be done. Abraham had done everything *he* could possibly do. He passed all ten tests. But the final firming up of God's covenant came at a later time. It came when Isaac passed the torch to Jacob. We explain the meaning of that delay and the logic behind it.

The three qualifications that Abraham needed to demonstrate were obedience, belief, and commitment to transmission. The first two characteristics are indications of his personality traits, demonstrated by his behavior when tested.

But the third characteristic was more complicated. Abraham needed to demonstrate commitment to the mission of transmission. We saw through several tests that he was behaviorally committed to this mission. But transmission requires a transmitter and a receiver. The receiver needs to be as serious about the role as Abraham was about his. Also, they both need to be successful in their role. That is, the receiver must accept what is taught. How do we know if the transmitter worked hard enough to achieve this task? A transmitter achieves success by demonstrating that one of his or her receivers has become a transmitter. For commitment to transmission to be demonstrated, the receiver must accept the content of what is being transmitted and in turn demonstrate successful transmission.

Abraham's role of transmitter could not be complete until he trained Isaac to be a transmitter. And we could not know that Isaac was successful until he successfully trained at least one of his children in the word of God. It would only be at that point that Abraham's job would be done.

Why is one full generation's demonstration of commitment to transmission adequate? It does not guarantee that the transmission will continue forever. Of course, God could not expect a demonstration of infinite transmissions. But He insisted that one generation of successful transmission take place (see *Yoma* 2a, mishnah 1:1). Was that sufficient? We know from Deuteronomy (31:21) that God knows the Torah will never be forgotten from the Jewish people (see Rashi, Deuteronomy 31:21, s.v. "*ki lo*"). We don't know the mysteries of how God works or what God knows, but with the full demonstration of transmission, God can assure that the Torah will never be forgotten.

Consider, also, the verse in which we learned the importance of transmission. God says about Abraham "that he may command his children" (18:19). That's the teaching part of transmission. Abraham achieved that in his lifetime. But the verse continues, "and his household after him that they may keep the way of the Lord to do righteousness and justice." It is not sufficient to teach. It is necessary that the lessons be absorbed, learned, implemented, and re-taught. The necessity to transmit to one more generation is a logical conclusion that has textual support as well.

Indeed, Abraham transmitted to everyone. He transmitted to Eliezer, Isaac, Lot, Ishmael, the sons of Keturah, and the souls he inspired in Charan. But not all of these succeeded in the sense that transmission continued to further generations. This emphasizes the point that Abraham's full demonstration of being a transmitter needed to wait until Isaac became a transmitter.

It is important to clarify the distinction between commitment to transmission and the other two attributes (obedience and belief). First, clearly Isaac had those attributes as well – indeed, at some level he was tested for those at the "binding" at the same time that Abraham was tested. But the need to test Isaac for commitment to transmission was unique. Even Abraham could not be said to have been successfully tested for commitment to transmission insofar as he didn't know if Isaac himself would transmit. Without Isaac demonstrating success, even Abraham's attempts would not count as successes.

The main thesis of this book is to demonstrate how belief, obedience, and commitment to transmission are the key qualifications for the Chosen People. We demonstrated this by the observation that the Torah calls out these qualities in Abraham. We also demonstrated this by observing that the ten tests actually tested for these qualifications.

Here, in the analysis of Esau, we see yet another demonstration that commitment to transmission is a critical qualifier. Our quandary was to understand exactly when the Patriarchs were certified. If they were certified prior to Isaac starting a family (e.g., when Abraham passed his tenth test), then there was no way to explain why Esau was excluded while sinning descendants of Jacob were included. If they were not certified prior to Isaac starting a family, then we struggled to find an event that provides the final qualifier. The only thing that stands out as the qualifier – and the explanation as to why Jacob was included and Esau could not be – is Isaac's successful transmission to Jacob. And as we will see in the next chapter, there is also textual support to that timing of the final certification.

With that as overall guidance, the next chapter will provide a complete analysis of Isaac's life and demonstrate how it completes the anatomy of the Chosen People.

Pre-Tested at the Binding of Isaac

While the key test was for Isaac to demonstrate commitment to transmission, in some sense, Isaac was tested for belief and obedience at the binding of Isaac (Genesis chapter 22). While the Torah characterizes it as a test of Abraham (22:1), the simple reading of the text implies that it was a test of Isaac as well.

We don't know exactly when Isaac figured out that he would be placed on the altar. Did Abraham tell him at the beginning? Was he told in the middle?

Did Isaac figure it out himself? But at some point, he figured it out. Let's trace his growing realization of what was happening. There is no sign through 22:6 that Isaac understood what was amiss. But in 22:7, Isaac already asks where the offering is, and in 22:8, Abraham mysteriously indicates that God will point out the offering. It seems that Isaac's suspicions are aroused.

Even if Isaac did not figure out Abraham's plan at 22:7, he figured it out soon thereafter. In 22:9, Isaac is bound to the altar. In 22:10, Abraham takes the knife. There is no other offering around. Isaac at that point must realize that in his father's mind, he himself might be the offering.

Isaac does not protest. He passes the test.

One can easily argue that this was a greater test for Isaac than it was for Abraham. Abraham had a long-standing relationship with God extending over decades of prophecy. He had received a direct commandment from God to take Isaac. On the other hand, we have no record that God spoke to Isaac at all prior to the binding. Moreover, Isaac did not receive a direct commandment to be the sacrificial lamb for Abraham's ordeal. Despite the lack of clear confirmation that this was the right path, Isaac believed in God and trusted his father, truly passing this test.

Commentaries indicate that Isaac's acceptance came even earlier in the story. Verse 22:8 says, "So they went both of them together." Radak interprets that to mean that they were with one heart. Isaac was willing to sacrifice his own life if that were God's wish.

According to tradition (see Rashi 23:2), the shock of the news of the binding of Isaac caused Sarah's death at age 127. Thus, Isaac was an adult of approximately thirty-seven years of age when the binding happened. He was not a small child tricked into accepting his fate. He was a fully grown, mature man who willingly accepted.

Let's examine the implications of this being a test for Isaac as well.

We developed in chapter 2 that the binding of Isaac was Abraham's "final exam." It incorporated elements of testing for belief, obedience, and the mission of transmission. Arguably, it was also the hardest test given what God was asking Abraham to do. While Abraham's battery of tests built up to this one hardest test, Isaac was experiencing it as his first test. Immediately, at age thirty-seven, he was tested on belief and obedience. But he had not yet illustrated any success at transmission.

Marriage and Children – The Ultimate Test

Genesis chapter 24 is one of the longest chapters in the Torah, with sixty-seven verses. It is dedicated entirely to Abraham's servant Eliezer finding Rebecca as Isaac's mate. Given the small number of verses associated with Isaac's life overall, it is astonishing that so much text is dedicated to this effort. Why?

In chapter 1, we discussed the mission of transmission as a family effort. Given that the overarching goal for Isaac's life was to demonstrate success at the mission of transmission, it becomes clear why this search for a mate was so central. The mission went beyond educating the world in the ways of God. It was to establish a clan – which was to become the Chosen People – who would aspire to a higher level of commitment and thereby be role models to following in God's ways.

The central element of making that plan successful was a couple working together. Just as Abraham and Sarah were partners in the establishment of the clan, Isaac needed a worthy partner. We see in almost all the key vignettes of Isaac's life that his wife Rebecca was an essential partner. Her role is more obvious than Sarah's. In vignette after vignette, she is the guiding hand that ensures that transmission to Jacob is successful. Since parenting is a joint project of father and mother, and Isaac's major project was to transmit to his children, the importance of selecting the right spouse was paramount.

Much of the chapter (24:12–25) emphasizes Rebecca's *middot* (positive character traits). Evidently, a woman of good *middot* is an appropriate candidate for the Matriarch position and transmitter of the mission. A person with fine character traits quickly becomes a role model whom others want to emulate.

The conclusion of Genesis chapter 24 emphasizes that the search is related to Rebecca's role as a Matriarch focused on the mission of transmission: "And Isaac brought her into his mother Sarah's tent" (24:67). Rebecca was to be the new Sarah. She needed to fulfill the role that Sarah had played in the previous generation. Famously, Sarah was involved in the transmission of the word of God to everyone (Rashi 12:5). Rashi (24:67) emphasizes that Rebecca became the image of Sarah. Given that Sarah was known as the expert in transmission (Rashi 12:5), this implies that Rebecca must have filled those shoes well.

Aside from the initial verification at the binding that Isaac would be a worthy successor for belief and obedience, the major task Isaac had left was to demonstrate effectiveness at transmission. As we said above, without his passing that test, it would turn out that even Abraham had not fully achieved transmission.

Isaac's test went beyond successfully mentoring the next worthy child, the next Patriarch – Jacob. The mission to transmit the Torah does not stop at "transmitting to the best student." The mission is to transmit to *everyone*. Even the weakest student. Even the one who misbehaves. Yes, even to Esau. Part of his test was to do everything he could to bring Esau into the covenant. We will see extraordinary efforts performed by Isaac to achieve that goal.

Although Isaac had the additional test of *attempting* to transmit to Esau, Isaac was not required to succeed with Esau – the teacher does not get to select his students, and not every student will learn. But he was obligated to try.

Isaac would have preferred to succeed with both children. He had no reason to assume that one would succeed and one would fail. He knew that his half brother Ishmael was not included in the covenant. But that was because Ishmael came from a different mother, who was not a life partner in a godly mission. He also knew that Ishmael exhibited some improper behaviors (see chapter 5). And he saw how distraught Abraham was that Ishmael was not included (see chapter 2). Isaac assumed that both his sons, twins from the same mother, would be part of the Chosen People.

With that understanding, we can appreciate the interaction between Isaac and Esau throughout their lives. A major subtheme of chapters 25–28 is Isaac's attempts – against all odds – to transmit the path of God to Esau.

It begins in the womb. God tells Rebecca that the stirring of the children in her womb represents that she will birth two nations (25:23). The dichotomy between Isaac's desire to bring both children into the covenant and the very different nature of these children appears from the beginning.

Rashi (25:23, s.v. "*mime'ayich*") is conflicted about the identity and nature of these two nations, explaining that one will be righteous and one will be wicked. We presume that Jacob is the righteous one and Esau the wicked one. But remarkably, Rashi hints (ibid., s.v. "*shnei goyim*") that both nations could have redeeming features. Rashi explains that the two nations refer to the great Jewish scholar Rebbe and to the Roman emperor Antoninus (presumably descended from Esau), who befriended Rebbe and is spoken of highly by the

Sages (*Avodah Zarah* 10b). What is Rashi's message? The first explanation
points to Esau's wickedness and the second to his potential. Good can come
from Esau.

Also illuminating is Chizkuni's commentary on Rashi's statement that one
would be righteous and one wicked. Chizkuni states that in the womb, it was
not yet known which would be which. This contravenes our intuition, which
tells us that Jacob was destined for righteousness and Esau for wickedness.
How else to read that it was already known that the two would choose different paths? Yet Chizkuni – interpreting Rashi – implies that both had potential for righteousness. And if they both had potential, certainly Isaac would
need to treat both as potential successors in the godly mission.

This uncertainty about who will ultimately be good or evil – or could they
both be good, like Rebbe and Antoninus? – is our first clue of the test or challenge of Isaac's mission. The parent never knows how the children will turn
out. It is not predestined. And it is not up to the parent. There are too many
factors. Isaac's job was to *attempt* transmission to both.

Our Sages oddly introduce two other characters into this vignette. When
God tells Rebecca the prophecy about the boys in 25:23, He does not speak
directly to Rebecca. He communicates with her either through Abraham
(Chizkuni, Ibn Ezra, Radak) or Shem (Rashi, Radak). These were the two
stalwarts who understood the mission of transmission: Abraham, who recognized that the ultimate measure of his life's goal would be Isaac's commitment
and success at transmitting the word of God to these two children, and Shem,
who could have been a Patriarch but failed at the critical piece of transmission.

What are these characters doing in this vignette? It is as if the Torah is
saying that the prophecy of the "two nations" is not about the fate of the two
boys. The prophecy foreshadows that their birth is setting up Isaac's test about
transmission. The foreshadowing is accomplished by bringing in Abraham
and Shem, who are very aware of the importance of that test.

Abraham shows up in another dimension of the Esau story. The transmission to Esau and Jacob was going to be Isaac's task, not Abraham's. Although
the latter was alive when his grandchildren were born, the two boys were not
easily distinguishable (in deed) until Abraham died (Ramban 25:27). Isaac
needed to be the one to pass the mantle to the next generation.

In summary, the early childhood of Isaac's children sets up the lifelong imperative and challenge for Isaac to attempt to transmit the way of God to his children.

How Isaac Demonstrated Transmission

Once the children are born, the Torah gives little detail about the actual relationship between Isaac and his children. We only have the following:

- Two verses (25:27–28) say that Esau was a hunter whom Isaac loved, and Jacob was a dweller in tents whom Rebecca loved. This happened when they were thirteen years old (and Isaac was seventy-three).
- One verse (26:35) reports that Esau's Canaanite wives embittered the lives of Isaac and Rebecca. Esau was forty (26:34), so Isaac was one hundred.
- The long chapter 27 treats Isaac's blessings to his children. Rashi (27:2) tells us that Isaac was 123 years old.

For Isaac, whose main task was the mission of transmission, there is a great deal missing. We have often asked about Genesis why it contains long stories with extensive digressions. What is the Torah trying to teach when it goes into such detail? Here, we have the opposite issue: there is so little text.

Basic analysis shows, however, that little text is needed for the Torah to convey its point. Isaac carefully reared his children until they were thirteen. When Jacob reached this age, the task of assuring he would have a career of Torah study was achieved. The Torah reports that Jacob sat in tents (25:27). Rashi explains that these were the tents of the two great teachers of that day, Shem and Ever. (It is somewhat interesting that this great achievement of transmission was not "owned" by Isaac alone, as he relied on these ancestors. But presumably, as the father, he was always involved in transmission to Jacob.) Nothing else needed to be done. The mission was well established. Jacob had taken to Torah study and loved the lifestyle. Isaac had the success he needed for his final test. Jacob would eagerly learn and transmit the word of God.

The proof text that Isaac has completed the test appears immediately in the next chapter of Genesis. There is a famine (26:1), and God appears to Isaac (26:2). He tells him that all promises made to Abraham will be passed on to

Isaac and his descendants (26:3). Isaac's descendants will be numerous, will inherit the land, and will be the source of blessing for all nations (26:4). Then God gives the reason for these promises (26:5). It is because Abraham listened to God. We will soon argue that this is the moment when transmission has its final demonstration. Since demonstration of multigenerational transmission was the last remaining item to be tested for, the role of the Patriarchs as the progenitors of the Chosen People has been sealed.

Many commentaries say that "listened to God" (26:5) refers to the binding of Isaac. This is a logical inference. After all, the binding of Isaac was Abraham's final exam. But why did God choose *this* moment to appear to Isaac to report that this was the key credit? After all, the binding of Isaac happened thirty-five or forty years earlier. Why not appear to Isaac right after the binding? Or when he married Rebecca? Or when he had children?

One explanation is that God appeared to Isaac soon after Abraham's death (when Isaac was seventy-five). With Abraham's passing, God needed to formally pass the torch to Isaac as the lead Patriarch of his day, and this was achieved with the blessing of chapter 26.

But here is a different explanation that makes the timing of this revelation precise. Rashi does not mention the binding of Isaac in 26:5. According to Rashi in 26:5, God made the promises to Abraham because he passed the tests. We have argued that Abraham's tests were not fully passed until *Isaac* was able to demonstrate the success of transmission. That happened at this exact time! The moment when Jacob reached age thirteen was when it was demonstrated that Isaac was successful and hence Abraham was *fully* successful. That is a direct and specific explanation why God appeared to Isaac at that very moment – it was God informing Isaac that the overall patriarchal mission had succeeded.

More succinctly, the Torah informs us that Isaac has succeeded in the mission of transmission. Jacob has accepted the mission. God comes to Isaac to close the loop – the baton has been passed. The long testing regimen, lasting over a hundred years, has been completed.

There is another textual clue to support the assertion that with Isaac's transmission to Jacob, the testing is complete. Jacob was born when Isaac was 60 and Abraham 160. When Jacob reached age 13, Isaac was 73 and Abraham 173. Roughly two years later, Abraham died (25:8). At his death, the Torah describes Abraham as "in a good old age." It seems that the goodness is the completion of his mission, which had just happened. Indeed, Radak lists his grandchildren as one element of Abraham's good life.

The tests for transmission have been satisfied with Isaac's transmitting to Jacob (26:5). Parenthetically, it is important to recognize that Jacob was a transmitter as well. Rashi explains that Jacob used to study with his son Joseph before he was kidnapped (45:27). Later, Jacob went further by transmitting to his grandson Ephraim (Rashi 48:1).

The success of transmitting to Jacob is a critical moment in the establishment of the Chosen People. All of Abraham's good intentions would be for naught if Isaac could not continue the transmission. It is only in 26:5 that the covenant has been sealed.

Hypothetically, if Isaac had failed to interest either of his sons in this divine mission, then the original goal of setting up a dynasty starting with Abraham would be lost. There would be no one to continue the mission. And from the perspective of qualifications, Abraham would have failed to demonstrate that his attempts at transmission were successful. God would have needed to find a different starting point for the Chosen People.

In Ecclesiastes (4:12), King Solomon says that "a three-stranded cord will not quickly be broken." Rashi explains that the three-stranded cord refers to a person who is a scholar, his son, and his grandson. With such merit, the Torah will never cease from his seed, as it says in Isaiah (59:21). This again emphasizes that transmission is considered successful only when the initial receiver (Isaac in this case) can both receive and successfully transmit.

The Love between Isaac and Esau

A significant fraction of the narrative of Isaac's life is about his love for Esau. We will discuss:

- The reasons for Isaac's dedication to Esau
- How Esau returned the love
- How it relates to Isaac's dedication to the mission of transmission

Isaac's love for Esau needs explanation, because superficially Esau is the evil son, and it would be hard to understand why Isaac has such a great love for him.

The problems began in the womb. Jacob and Esau struggled with each other (25:22). Rashi explains that Esau was anxious to leave the womb to engage in idolatry. It seems that Esau was destined for evil.

As they grew, they developed different natures. Esau was a hunter (25:27). Rashi explains that he hunted and tricked Isaac. Ibn Ezra says that he was sly, because without the ability to fool, you can't hunt. Jacob by contrast was a quiet man, dwelling in tents (ibid.). As mentioned above, Rashi explains that this refers to Torah study in the academies of Shem and Ever.

Despite Esau's bad character, the Torah tells us that Isaac loved Esau, but Rebecca loved Jacob (25:28).

Esau's character deficiencies go from bad to worse. In 25:29, Esau is tired, and Rashi explains that he is fatigued from his murderous deeds. Jacob offers to feed his tired brother in exchange for his birthright. Esau in accepting this bargain reasons that it is a good deal, because after all, Esau will die (25:31). Commentaries have alternative pejorative interpretations of Esau's reasoning. According to Rashi, the birthright is service to God, and Esau rejects it. According to Chizkuni, it is the promise to inherit Canaan. Esau rejects it because the inheritance occurs after four hundred years (15:14–16), and by then Esau himself will be dead. In either case, he is portrayed in a negative light.

To complete the rejection, the Torah explains that Esau despised the birthright (25:34).

Finally, when Esau marries, his wives fill the household with bitterness (26:35). Rashi explains that the bitterness was idolatry.

Despite all of Esau's negative character traits, Isaac loves him. And when it comes to the final blessings (chapter 27), Isaac's first instincts are that the primary blessings go to Esau. What is going on?

When we recall Isaac's mission in life, the entire relationship with Esau becomes far more understandable.

Isaac knew that his job was to continue the traits of belief and obedience, and most importantly to transmit God's ways to the next generation. His life story is the attempt to achieve that.

Isaac had every reason to assume that he was expected to transmit to *all* of his children. He saw his father trying to transmit to Ishmael even though he was not born to Sarah. Certainly, in Isaac's case, where both sons came from the Matriarch Rebecca, it would have been reasonable to assume that both should be included in the covenant.

There was however no guarantee that either would be in the covenant. Abraham could not complete the job of demonstrating transmission, as discussed above. That was Isaac's job. This was the critical generation. Any child of Isaac who accepted the mantle of transmission would be part of the covenant, and any child who didn't would be outside. If neither child accepted, God would need to find a different family to start with.

While Isaac's twins were in the womb, God gave Rebecca a cryptic message: "one people shall be stronger than the other people; and the elder shall serve the younger" (25:23). It's unclear whether Rebecca ever shared this with Isaac. But even if she did, what would he make of it? It seems to be about temporal matters. It does not condemn either to be outside the covenant. Isaac continued to believe that they would both be included.

The critical verse is "Now Isaac loved Esau" (25:28). This could be understood at many levels. At the most basic level, it is a father loving a son, despite his faults.

Commentaries downgrade that love. Radak says that Isaac loved Esau, but loved Jacob even more. Chizkuni explains that Isaac only loved Esau when he was feeding him.

But with our insight that Isaac's job was to mentor all his children, there is a more natural explanation. Despite Esau's faults, Isaac had every expectation that in the end, he would be on the right path. Isaac saw that with his half brother Ishmael. Abraham never gave up on Ishmael, and in the end, Ishmael repented (Rashi 25:9).

Thus, Isaac truly loved Esau. He would not banish his son. His love for Esau was more than the love of a father. It was the love of a father who was certain that every miscue was a passing mistake, but that ultimately Esau would repent. They would remain in each other's lives. Isaac would continually extol to Esau how wonderful he was as a great hunter. He was building a relationship with Esau – not trying to send him off. He would never despair of his goal to include Esau in the Chosen People. Yes, Isaac did not need to continue with Esau if he only wanted to fulfill the minimal requirement of transmission. Isaac achieved the requirement with his successful raising of Jacob. But Isaac was dedicated to the broader mission and wanted to do more.

Isaac maintained that faith until the very end – he felt he could succeed; he felt he needed to succeed.

We can take this to another level. Let's recall that the characteristic Isaac needed to excel in was to demonstrate the mission of transmission. With hindsight, the son who would transmit was the saintly Jacob, who was a scholar sitting in tents. We associate hunters like Esau with base human characteristics and trickery. That is why it is hard for us to intuit why Isaac loved him.

But Isaac might have looked at it differently. A transmitter is an activist, someone who goes out and engages with the world. The original transmitter was Abraham, a great fighter who participated in and won the battle of the nine kings. (There is no record that Isaac himself was much of a fighter.) When Isaac saw his two sons, he saw one (Esau) who was outgoing, a man of the world, with the right personality to be a leader and a transmitter. As a father, he overlooked the faults. He might have thought that Esau was more likely to be a transmitter than the bookish Jacob, who never left the tent. The mission of transmission required an evangelist's attention to outreach.

Alternatively, we can follow the path of the Malbim (27:1). In that formulation, Isaac never intended for Esau to receive a spiritual blessing; indeed, the entire blessing intended for Esau talks about material wealth. In this formulation, Isaac foresaw a partnership between Esau and Jacob. Jacob necessarily would carry the spiritual mantle. But if Jacob were focused entirely on the spiritual, reasoned Isaac, then who would provide for his physical needs? So Isaac anticipated that Esau would provide physical sustenance as part of a partnership with Jacob, the spiritual leader. The Malbim also points out that this is not very different from the situation one generation later – the tribe of Levi takes on the spiritual responsibility, and the rest of the tribes provide sustenance to the Levites.

The Torah continues the sparse description of Isaac's family. We next encounter Esau and Isaac in 26:34–35. The Torah relates that at age forty, Esau took two Hittite women as wives, and their behavior caused bitterness to Isaac and Rebecca. What is the Torah's point with this vignette?

The commentaries are uniformly critical of everyone for these two verses.

- Sforno criticizes Isaac that he did not seek a proper marriage for his sons (as Abraham did when Isaac reached forty).
- Sforno also criticizes Esau for taking Hittite women.
- Radak criticizes Esau for taking these women.
- Rashi explains that Esau had many previous promiscuous relationships.
- Rashi also explains that the women were idolators.

But while these commentaries explain what is happening – why Esau is now taking wives, why they are bad, what mistakes were being made – these commentaries do not explain why the Torah bothers to share this information with us.

Rashbam explains the purpose of the verses. Rashbam explains that these verses are setting up the future situation in which Jacob will leave Canaan to find a wife. These verses are a counterpoint to the appropriate way that Jacob will wed, and they explain his departure from Canaan. While this is an explanation, it is not compelling. After all, Abraham sent Eliezer to Charan to find a wife for Isaac. The Torah could have just reported that Isaac similarly sent Jacob, following in his father's footsteps. There was no need to report on Esau's wives.

Let us suggest a different theory. The story of the Patriarchs is the explanation of how they demonstrated the key characteristics that qualified them as progenitors of the Chosen People. We can understand these verses to be part of Isaac's qualifiers as follows.

Isaac never rejected Esau. He remained committed throughout his life to do all he could to train Esau in the ways of God. Isaac understood Esau's limitations. He appreciated that Esau's behaviors were not what they needed to be, but he did not give up. When Esau married women who only caused bitterness, Isaac – unlike his father Abraham – did not banish his child. He swallowed the bitterness to ensure that the family bonds persisted. The purpose of these verses is to highlight that Esau would not suffer the fate of Ishmael, due to Isaac's complete commitment to his mission.

In a peculiar way, Esau returned the favor. As a forty-year-old hunter who had married the daughters of notables, he had every opportunity to desert his hundred-year-old father and live his life on his own terms. But he could not do that. He remained dedicated to his parents. How else to explain why he was even around their house at this stage in his life? Esau and Isaac could never understand each other, but they each tried to make the relationship work.

The centerpiece to understanding Isaac's attitudes toward his sons is Genesis chapter 27, when Isaac brings Esau in for a blessing. The complexity of these blessings will be explained soon; here, we focus on Esau's reaction.

Briefly, the blessings had been a disaster for Esau. In 27:28–29, Jacob received the extraordinary blessings that Isaac had intended for Esau. In 28:4, Jacob received the other extraordinary blessing that Isaac had reserved for Jacob. With Esau standing there in bitterness (27:34) and tears (27:38), Isaac finally gave Esau a lesser blessing (27:39–40). Esau was consumed with rage against Jacob (27:41).

Interestingly, the sixty-three-year-old Esau was not enraged with the 123-year-old Isaac. He could have been. It was Isaac's carelessness that caused this disaster for Esau. Isaac could have simply woken up one day and blessed Esau without sending him out to prepare a tasty meal. Isaac could have worked harder to ascertain the identity of who came back for the blessings. But we see no trace of hatred toward Isaac on Esau's part.

This is a continuation of the pattern of Isaac and Esau's relationship. Esau could have been angry with his father. He wasn't. Esau could have been resigned – he could have left Isaac in frustration. After all, as a successful, married, middle-aged hunter, he didn't need to kowtow to his father at all. He didn't leave. Instead, with some introspection, he tried to understand where his father was coming from.

The Torah relates that Esau diagnosed the root cause of the problem with his father (28:6). Esau had married a Canaanite woman, and his father disapproved. He took the criticism to heart and married his cousin Machalat (28:9) so he too would merit favor from his father.

But as we have seen throughout the relationship, he and his father were from different worlds. Superficially, Esau was doing the will of his father. But they didn't understand each other. Indeed, Rashi and Ramban both point out that if Esau really wanted a fresh start, he would have divorced the Hittite wives. Esau added an *additional* wife, which proves that although he ostensibly married Machalat to appease his father, his ulterior (and primary) motive was to satisfy his own desires.

Esau and Isaac never had a falling out despite their coming from different worlds. Isaac always reached out to Esau as a dedicated father. Esau could never meet expectations, but nevertheless continued the relationship until Isaac's burial (35:29).

After Jacob left Isaac for several decades to find wives and build a family, he returned to Canaan and was confronted by Esau. As he approached, Jacob feared the encounter (32:8). Chizkuni explains that Jacob was fearful because he was away from his parents and had not provided them with the proper honor and respect. It's odd that Jacob worried about his worthiness while confronting the evil Esau. With our new understanding of how much respect Esau afforded to Isaac despite their differences, we can better understand Jacob's fears. It was not only that Jacob had neglected the mitzvah, it was also that Esau was so dedicated to it. We can also understand why it was this particular mitzvah that Jacob was concerned about – it was the one mitzvah that Esau excelled at.

Isaac kept his hope about Esau throughout his life. It was only when it was revealed that Jacob had grabbed the blessings (27:33) that the Torah reports that Isaac trembled. Rashi explains that he saw Gehinnom (essentially, hell) open up – in other words, Esau's true self became clear. Chizkuni explains that Isaac reasoned as follows: How could God have allowed Jacob to get the blessing intended for Esau, unless it was Jacob who was truly deserving? He understood that Esau would never be deserving.

Once he saw the truth, Isaac appreciated that the true transmission would be through Jacob. He told Esau that he would serve his brother (27:40) and proceeded to give the blessing of Abraham to Jacob (28:4).

Chapter 8

The Blessings

The tension between Esau and Isaac – their desire to be a family, Isaac's desire to inculcate values into Esau, the fact that this could never work – comes to a head in the dramatic story of Isaac's blessings to his sons.

The story literally comes out of nowhere. An aging Isaac (123 years old by Rashi's calculation, 27:2) decides to bless Esau before he dies. He states it so matter-of-factly (27:4) that the reader is lulled into believing that deathbed blessings are routine and commonplace. Indeed, both Jacob (for his children) and Moses (for the twelve tribes) give extensive blessings as they near death. But Isaac's blessing is different. First, he is not near death – he has fifty-seven years to go (35:28). And this idea of bestowing blessings to one's children is novel. After all, Abraham gave everything to Isaac (25:5). But Rashi explains (25:11) that Abraham explicitly did *not* bless Isaac. Perhaps he deliberately did not bless Isaac, leaving blessings to God. Isaac must have had some specific objective when he set out to provide these blessings, and the Torah must have had some specific objective in reporting about them.

Isaac's Intentions
Isaac starts by inviting only Esau for a blessing (27:1). That, in and of itself, is strange. When Jacob later summons his children for their final blessings (Genesis chapter 49), he calls them together. That makes sense. Superficially, Isaac wants to bless only his eldest son Esau. Later (28:4), we learn that he had a two-stage plan – to first bless Esau and then to bless Jacob with the "blessing of Abraham."

From the story line, it appears that the blessing that Isaac was tricked into giving to Jacob (27:28–29) was the blessing that he had intended to give to Esau. Let's look at that blessing as we began to summarize at the beginning of the previous chapter and see what Isaac was thinking.

Verse 28 is simple enough. Isaac intends to bless Esau that he will accumulate wealth. Any father can want that for every one of his children.

Verse 29 is problematic. Isaac intends to bless Esau with "Let peoples serve you, and nations bow down to you." That is mildly problematic. Did Isaac understand Esau's immorality? Does he want the world saddled with an immoral ruler of Esau's type? Perhaps Isaac never appreciated the depths of Esau's moral turpitude.

But the next phrase in that verse is *majorly* problematic. "Be lord over your brethren, and let your mother's sons bow down to you." Isaac intends to give Esau physical dominion over Jacob. Why would he want to do something like that? What has Jacob done wrong? Is Isaac so out of touch about the relative nature of his sons that he thinks this is a good thing?

And Isaac meant this dominion literally. Later, Esau appears on the scene, hears what Jacob has done, and begs his father, "Have you not reserved a blessing for me?" (26:36). Isaac responds, "I have made him your lord" (26:37). Rashi explains that Isaac is implying, *What possible good could a blessing do for you, Esau? Since he is your lord, any property you gain becomes his.* In other words, the first blessing gives the acquirer of the blessing complete control over his brother. Since Jacob got the blessing, Esau is left with nothing. But considering that Isaac had intended that blessing for Esau, it means that his a priori wish was that Esau would get everything and Jacob nothing. This is inconceivable! And that is why it is very hard to understand Isaac's intentions.

The blessing intended for Esau cedes enormous authority to him. However, we must remember that Isaac had reserved a separate blessing for Jacob. To fully appreciate Isaac's intentions, we must look at those two blessings together.

Taken together, Isaac weaves a fascinating interdependence between his two sons which is targeted at assuring that the mission of living a godly life continues after Isaac's death. Let's look at the blessing intended for Jacob. In 28:4, Isaac asks God to give Jacob the "blessing of Abraham." He hadn't intended to give this to Esau in Genesis chapter 27; evidently, he was saving this for Jacob.

What was this blessing of Abraham? Several commentaries express that Jacob would be the heir who gets the blessings that God gave to Abraham.

Let's see what is involved in those blessings. We will focus on one key commitment that God made.

After the binding of Isaac, Abraham was promised, "and your seed shall possess the gate of his enemies" (22:17). By providing Jacob the "blessing of Abraham," Isaac bestows on Jacob the blessing of possessing the gate of his enemies.

Let's look at the two blessings together (that originally intended for Esau and that for Jacob). Each blessing provides a form of domination. The blessing intended for Esau provides domination over his brothers (interestingly plural in 27:29). The blessing for Jacob provides domination over his enemies.

That introduces a second problem with these blessings. First was the inconceivable – that Isaac intended to give domination to Esau over Jacob. Now there is an apparent contradiction between the two blessings: Which brother is dominating/possessing the other?

These two questions answer each other once we explain the extremely clever plan that Isaac created to ensure coexistence between Esau and Jacob after his own death.

There is a way to harmonize these two blessings so they are not contradictory. Jacob only rules over his *enemies*. If Esau is not an enemy of Jacob, Jacob has no dominion over him.

What does it take for Esau not to be an enemy of Jacob? He must follow in God's path. He must become part of the Chosen People. He must obey, believe, and transmit the message. That is all that Isaac ever wanted from Esau. His efforts were not succeeding. So in one sweeping move, at age 123, he tried to change the trajectory. He planned to offer Esau all that Esau could imagine, as a final "bribe" to turn Esau the right way.

Here was Isaac's plan. He would give *conflicting* blessings to his two sons. He would give nominal control to Esau. But he would tell him that the blessings nullify each other if Esau chooses to be an enemy of the Torah way of life. One blessing says that Esau will dominate his brother Jacob. But the other says that Jacob will possess his enemy Esau. If Esau is an enemy, the blessings cancel each other out. Esau gets nothing.

But if Esau chooses not to be an enemy – that is, if he chooses the Torah way of life – then he reaps all the physical blessings. In the physical domain, he gets everything.

Hirsch hints to this approach. In 27:29, where Isaac blesses with "be lord over your brethren," Hirsch says that Isaac does not mean to "bless" Esau as a "lord over Jacob." Rather, Hirsch explains the framing as "here is an opportunity or an imperative" – *if in addition to your material gains, you also obtain spiritual greatness, then Jacob will bow down before you.*

The Ohr Hachayim (27:1, s.v. *"beno hagadol"*) takes a similar path. He explains that Isaac's goal in blessing Esau was to get his wayward son on the correct path. In general, it pains righteous people to see their children performing evil deeds. So the notion that Isaac blessed Esau to keep him in the fold is not novel. To be clear, the Ohr Hachayim does not suggest that the convoluted interlocking blessings was the mechanism, but he is pointing to the general idea of correcting Esau's path.

Why would Isaac make Esau a lord over Jacob? It is a last desperate effort to ensure his legacy by transmitting Torah to both his sons – the achievement of a lifetime. He did the most he could possibly do to get Esau to agree.

Why would Isaac do this to Jacob? In truth, Jacob could have been agreeable to this. After all, in the spiritual domain, Jacob would have still been ascendant. He would have the blessing of Abraham. He might lack ownership of property, but he would have been protected by his friend and brother Esau. This could have been similar to the partnership between Zevulun the merchant and Issachar the scholar (Rashi 49:13). Losing physical property would be a small price to pay for the everlasting peace that would result, if indeed Esau turned to the good path.

Sforno (27:29) has a similar interpretation. He explains that enhancing Esau in the political sphere allows Jacob to more completely focus on the spiritual sphere. In essence, Esau becomes the physical protector of Jacob.

While Isaac had a clever plan to achieve all he wanted, God didn't sign on. Rebecca did not sign on. They both understood what Esau was made of. There was no scenario in which Esau would join the covenant. Setting up interlocking blessings, while clever, had no practical implication. Rebecca conspired to ensure that all the blessings went to Jacob.

Rabbi Samson Raphael Hirsch has a fascinating description of how the pieces fit together. In 27:1, Hirsch asks what Rebecca was trying to achieve from the beginning. After all, clearly the ruse would ultimately be discovered. Sooner or later, Isaac would learn that he blessed the wrong child. Once that happened, Isaac would withdraw the blessing from Jacob, give a blessing to Esau, and potentially curse Jacob for the treachery. We know Jacob had this concern from the outset (27:12). How could this possibly turn out well? Rebecca may not have understood why Isaac favored Esau, but that's the way it was.

Rabbi Hirsch explains that Rebecca understood everyone's motivations. Esau was sufficiently clever with his lifelong deception that Isaac could not believe he was irredeemable. Rebecca understood that Isaac would not recognize his error of having faith in Esau unless he could be shown how easy it was to be deceived. So she constructed her own elaborate deception, which Jacob carried out.

There is much to say about Jacob's behavior in all of this. After all, he clearly deceives his father – even lies to him about who he is when he comes for the blessing. Did he do the right thing in listening to the direct command of his mother, or does he deserve condemnation for being dishonest? Did he always deserve the blessings? After all, he had bought the firstborn privileges (25:33). Even if Jacob deserved the blessings, do the ends (receiving the blessing) justify the means (deception)? These and many other aspects of the life of Jacob (and later his children) deserve attention and scrutiny, but they are a bit off-topic for this book.

The ruse is revealed to Isaac, who trembles when he discovers that his plan went awry (27:33). Chizkuni explains Isaac's thought process. Isaac was not surprised that in his aged state with poor eyesight, he mistook Jacob for Esau. But he asks, how could God have let this happen? The only possible conclusion is that this was justice – Jacob deserved to get the blessings. Following Hirsch's reasoning, Rebecca finally succeeded in making Isaac realize that he was susceptible to being misled by Esau and that transmission would only go through Jacob.

Isaac's frustration shines through the narrative. Esau begs him for a blessing. Isaac has no response. Finally, he weakly says, "What shall I do for you, my son?" (27:37). He is stuck. He so much wanted his plan of interlocking blessings to work, yet God and Rebecca had conspired against him. (Rebecca's conspiring to prevent the blessings going to Esau is clear. In terms of God's role in the process, Rashi on 27:1, in his third explanation of the source of

Isaac's blindness, explains that the blindness was inflicted on him – presumably with divine intervention – to enable Jacob to get the blessings.)

Isaac's frustration over Esau was similar to what had happened to his father. At some point, Abraham realized that despite his efforts and love, the tradition would not pass through Ishmael (see chapter 2). Now Isaac faced the same reality: despite the fact that Esau had the same parents as Jacob, Esau would never enter the Chosen People. He had not accepted the mission of transmission. His opportunity had vanished.

Isaac was limited in what he could do for Esau (27:37). But he still loved his son. He also still hoped that Esau would display a modicum of morals. While God had given up on Esau for the Chosen People, Esau could still lead as good a life as his abilities would allow.

Apparently, Isaac struggled with this, because he actually gave Esau two different answers. First he said, "what then shall I do for you, my son" (27:37). In other words, Isaac was totally defeated. The elaborate interlock went away. There was nothing left for Esau.

After two verses, Isaac reversed himself. Finally, Isaac found a partial solution and blessed Esau. It is a blessing that reintroduces the interlock in a weaker fashion.

He starts by giving him a blessing for his material well-being, "the fat places of the earth, the dew of the heaven" (27:39). He speaks to Esau's values, extolling him as a man of the sword (27:40).

The end of the blessing is mysterious and meaningful. Isaac says, "when you shall break loose, that you shall shake his yoke off your neck" (27:40). It is not clear what he means when he says "when you shall break loose," but he appears to reference Esau being freed from Jacob.

Isaac has once again created tension and interplay between blessings. Originally, he planned to give Esau the upper hand, but only if he followed the path of God. Isaac lost that opportunity when Jacob received the blessing intended for Esau. But Isaac could still recover some of his original plan. Indeed, Jacob would get both the blessing intended for Esau as well as the "blessing of Abraham." But in Isaac's new plan, Esau's new blessing would make Jacob's domination conditional.

Isaac was determined to make the blessings interlock in order to assure a greater future of collaboration between his sons. Rebecca, Jacob, and God foiled his original plan, and he accepted that he had to change the strategy. But he continued with the general theme – only giving Esau less stature and control.

Commentaries differ on the exact conditioning that Isaac used.

- Rashi interprets "when you shall break loose" to mean when Jacob's descendants violate the Torah. In his interpretation, this phrase is a caution first and foremost to Jacob. He will lose his leadership role if he violates the Torah. Presumably, though, Esau needs to also follow the ways of God for him to achieve "shak[ing off the] yoke."
- Radak similarly explains that this is the result of Jacob's sins.
- Chizkuni explains that when Jacob's domination becomes oppressive, Esau will leave the Land of Israel and be independent outside of Israel.
- Ramban and Rashbam are similar to Chizkuni.

The emphasis in the commentaries is that the interplay is limited to misbehavior on Jacob's part. But with our understanding of Isaac's goal to have Esau also walk in God's path, it is reasonable to assume that Esau's descendants also needed to be of upstanding moral fiber to "shake [off the] yoke." Thus, although Jacob dominated Esau, Esau could regain his standing by leading a moral life.

In the original blessing that was intended for Esau (27:29), Esau would have been blessed that his brothers bow down to him – hence he would be dominant. The actual blessing that Esau received (27:40) says that Esau will be subservient to Jacob. The best it gets for Esau in this revised interlock is that he could break loose and shake off Jacob's yoke. So the revised interlock was weaker for Esau in two ways. First, for Esau to get something, Jacob had to sin. Second, even in that case, Esau would still not get domination.

It seems that God also supported Isaac's efforts to bring his son Esau into the fold. While we do not see God's involvement in the blessings, He does return to the Esau story at the end of the Torah.

After forty years of wandering in the desert, the freed Israelites are approaching the Land of Israel. In Deuteronomy 2:5, God cautions the Jews not to provoke the nation of Edom – the sons of Esau – because He has given them Mount Seir as an inheritance. It is remarkable that God deeds any land to anyone – let alone the descendants of a sinner. It seems that God also wants the descendants of Esau to form a cohesive nation – whether as a balance for Jacob or to bring them into the godly path. Whatever the precise reason, they are rewarded with a piece of land as their inheritance.

It is noteworthy that while this gesture is provided for Esau and Lot (see chapter 5), it is not provided for Ishmael or the other sons of Abraham.

This is an indication that God supported the idea of bringing Esau into the fold that is explicit in the Torah. But it is also interesting to see how our Sages weave it in throughout the story.

In 32:23, Rashi is discussing the confrontation between Jacob and Esau when Jacob returns to Canaan. He describes that Jacob hid his daughter Dina in a box so that Esau would not be attracted to her. He further says that part of Jacob's reasoning was a worry that Dina marrying Esau would lead him to the good path. Apparently, God did not approve of this, because Rashi continues that Jacob was punished (presumably by God) with Dina being taken by Shechem. God would have preferred to have Dina marry Esau and return him on the correct path.

Consequences of the Blessings

After Isaac adjusts his plans for the blessings, he finally takes stock of the broader picture. In 28:4, he gives to Jacob "the blessing of Abraham." It is only at that moment that Isaac himself is able to conclude (1) that the mission of transmission has been achieved, and (2) that it goes through Jacob alone.

As a prophet, Isaac understood the significance of identifying Jacob and passing the torch to him. When he blesses Jacob a second time and gives the Abrahamic blessing, he gives it "to you and your seed with you" (28:4). Hirsch explains that "your seed with you" is the statement that the test of transmission has been finalized – all of Jacob's seed are in the Chosen People.

But the confirmation of Jacob's ascension does not stop there. Until now, Jacob has not been spoken to directly by God. But the vignette that immediately follows Isaac's blessings and their aftermath has God conferring the same blessing to Jacob. As Jacob prepares to leave Canaan to find a wife, he has the dream of the ladder with angels. Then in 28:13, God introduces Himself as the God of Abraham and Isaac. This message is not coming from the persona of God as Creator of the universe – God's message is to point out the continuity of the patriarchal message.

God reviews the key aspects of the blessing in 28:13–15. The land will belong to Jacob and his descendants. His descendants will be numerous, and all the nations will be blessed by them. God will be with Jacob and fulfill the commitment.

The commentaries find extra echoes that the commitment to the Patriarchs is now sealed. Rashi (28:15) explains that He will not leave Jacob "until I have done that which I have spoken to you of." According to Rashi, this is God's indication to Jacob that all the promises made to Abraham and Isaac uniquely flow to Jacob and not to other descendants.

There is an interesting passage in I Chronicles 16:16–17, which recounts that God established a covenant with Abraham and swore to Isaac. It appears that God's relationship with Abraham and Isaac is of one form – dealing with them as individuals and promising about the future. But then it says that God established this with Jacob to be an everlasting covenant. The medieval commentator Ralbag points out that this is a commitment that will never leave Jacob (i.e., his descendants). Could this be a textual confirmation that until Jacob, there was an iota of possibility that the covenant could still have been changed, if Abraham and Isaac did not complete the testing battery?

When Jacob wakes up from his vision, he plays back to God what he heard. He promises that if God keeps His commitment, he will be loyal in return: "and the Lord will be my God" (28:21). Rashi has a fascinating interpretation of that statement. Jacob is understanding that God's name will rest on Jacob from beginning to end. By this he means that no descendant of Jacob will be disqualified. Jacob infers this from 28:15.

In other words, Jacob interprets this blessing from God to go beyond the blessings to Abraham and Isaac. Jacob understands that at this very moment, God has made the commitment that *all* of Jacob's descendants will be part of the covenant – unlike the situation with Abraham and Isaac, who had descendants who were *not* part of the covenant. The reason this is communicated to Jacob at this very moment is that this is the exact moment when Esau's destiny has been revealed. Isaac saw that his efforts to include Esau had failed. He saw Gehinnom open before him. It was time to communicate it to Jacob as well.

What about Esau? The simple explanation is that Esau could have merited to be a Patriarch and part of the Chosen People. But Esau needed to demonstrate being a capable receiver of the tradition from Isaac. He failed. And so he is not part of the Chosen People. Since the covenants were not sealed until Isaac demonstrated transmission, Esau did not automatically enter into the covenant.

On the other hand, once the covenants with the forefathers were complete, any future descendant (i.e., descendant of Jacob), is automatically part of the Chosen People. Even a sinner is not rejected from the covenant.

Chapter 9

Rebecca's Centrality

In chapter 4, we discussed that Sarah was an equal partner to Abraham. Although the style of the Torah places Abraham in the middle of most of the events, nonetheless, there were clues in the text and commentary that the covenantal mission was for the entire family – Matriarchs and Patriarchs – and not limited to males.

Rebecca is more central to the storyline of Genesis than the other Matriarchs. While Sarah is a participant in the Abraham narrative, her role is often understated, and she is totally missing from key vignettes. Rebecca, by contrast, is active in almost every story. She plays a different role than does Isaac. Often, she is the spouse whose alignment with God's wishes is most clear. She is a role model for women through the ages, including our own.

It is not surprising how central Rebecca is, given how much effort was expended to locate this worthy spouse (see chapter 5). She was extensively vetted before being selected. Isaac brought her home, and she immediately picked up Sarah's foundational role.

It is interesting to think about this from the broader perspective of Isaac's life. In Genesis chapter 22, Isaac has a traumatic experience – he is apparently being taken as a sacrifice. Let's look at Isaac's life in the wake of that event.

In 22:5, Abraham had told the two lads that were accompanying him and Isaac that after going to Mount Moriah, he and Isaac would return. Isaac appears to be agreeable to this, because in both 22:6 and 22:8, the Torah says that Abraham and Isaac went together. Yet at the end of the vignette, in 22:19, only Abraham returns to the two lads. Isaac is missing. Apparently, the entire incident had an understandably crushing impact on Isaac.

Isaac's absence continues in the next chapters. Shockingly, he is completely absent from chapter 23 when his mother is buried. This is the mother who waited so long for his birth and who protected him from the bad influences of Ishmael. Yet Isaac could not even attend the funeral and burial.

Genesis chapter 24 is the lengthy description of Eliezer locating Rebecca and bringing her to Canaan. Isaac is missing until the end of the story. This thirty-seven-year-old man has no role in the discussions about how his mate will be chosen.

When Rebecca arrives, Isaac recognizes that it is a good match. He brings her home. She is the matron of the house. Isaac is comforted.

Actually, Rebecca's vetting started at her birth. The commentaries explain that the purpose of 22:20–24 is principally to show Rebecca's lineage. Sforno goes as far as suggesting that the events of these verses signaled to Abraham that there was now a suitable match for Isaac.

The entire early life of Isaac is narrated by the Torah and seen through the eyes of Abraham. The only words that Isaac contributes are on the way to his binding: he asks, "Where is the ram?" (22:7). The Sages see him as praiseworthy to go along with the binding, but there is no expression of his personality.

Rebecca is introduced in the opposite manner.

Abraham sends Eliezer to Charan to find a wife (24:4), and according to Radak, indicates to Eliezer that Rebecca is the intended target. When Eliezer encounters Rebecca, the Torah attests to Rebecca's modest behavior (24:16), her kindness (24:17–20), and her directness in responding to questions (Rashi 24:24). She willingly and excitedly agrees to join the godly family (24:58). She approaches Isaac with modesty (24:65).

This introduction is capped off in 24:67. What did we expect when Isaac and Rebecca were brought together? We might have expected that Rebecca, who grew up in the house of idolators, would be the one who is transformed. We would expect that by moving into the holy home of the Patriarchs, she would learn the ways of God. But that didn't happen – because it didn't need to happen. She was already God-fearing. The transformation worked the other way. With Rebecca in the house fulfilling the role of Sarah, Isaac was consoled and started to come out of his shell.

In their life together, Isaac and Rebecca are usually paired, such as when Isaac prays for Rebecca to have children (25:21). But the next vignette involves only Rebecca. It is a difficult pregnancy, and she asks God for direction (25:22). God reveals to her alone that there are two nations in her womb who will have different destinies (25:23). Rashbam learns from this that God favored Jacob, which is why Rebecca favored Jacob (25:28). Chizkuni learns that Jacob will dominate Esau. Inexplicably, Isaac favors the son who will not lead a proper life (Esau), but Rebecca's instincts draw her to the saintly son Jacob.

Ramban (27:4) tries to understand how Isaac could have possibly wanted to give Esau the primary blessings. He concludes that Rebecca never told Isaac about the prophecy of "the elder shall serve the younger" (25:23). Ramban interprets this verse to mean that Jacob is the son whom God favors. Ramban continues and says that Isaac would never knowingly have blessed Esau if he knew of the prophecy. Doing so would be tantamount to violating God's will.

Ramban's view that this prophecy went to Rebecca and not Isaac – that Rebecca never told Isaac, and the latter indeed never knew about it – is stunning. Isaac was the Patriarch. He was the son of Abraham. Why would God share this information with Rebecca and not with Isaac? What was the purpose of sharing this information with Rebecca altogether?

This vignette provides insight on both Isaac's and Rebecca's roles.

Recall Isaac's mission in life. He needed to demonstrate commitment to the transmission of God's way of life, particularly to his children. That was the major test of his life.

It was critical for Isaac to *not* know what would be the fate of his children. Advanced knowledge of their fate would get in the way of his working on his major test. How could he work on transmitting the Torah to Jacob if he already knew that the endeavor would be successful? Sure, he would still teach the Torah to him. But the mystery would be gone if success was guaranteed. Perhaps Isaac would lose some of the passion for the task, if he knew that it was not in doubt. Could it even be called a test, in that case?

It was also critical that he *not* know that Esau would not stay on the right path. As we have seen, Isaac dedicated his life to keeping Esau within the fold. That this was such a hard task allowed Isaac to show his dedication at a superlative level. Had Isaac known of its ultimate futility, he could not possibly have worked at the same level. It would have unfairly removed an opportunity to demonstrate his fidelity.

This also allowed Isaac to be deceived, however. Esau was a master of deception (Rashi 25:28). Isaac never really appreciated how irredeemable Esau was. That caused Isaac to intend to bless Esau with domination over Jacob (27:4

and 29). Isaac did not realize that a hurting, angry Esau might plan to rise and kill Jacob (27:41). He needed eyes and ears to appreciate the situation.

Rebecca comes into her own in the story about the blessings of the children. Isaac has his plan to provide a blessing to Esau. Rebecca determines that Isaac's plan is wrong. Esau does not deserve the blessing, which should rather go to Jacob. Rebecca choreographs a different approach to alter the path of history that she knew was right – against the expressed desires of her husband.

She is an activist. She expresses her vision to Jacob not as a "plan," but as a commandment (27:8). She assigns Jacob the menial task of finding two good goats, but she takes on the task to prepare the food for Isaac (27:9). She commands Jacob to trick his father into giving the blessings (27:10).

Jacob is concerned that the plot will be discovered and he will be cursed (27:11). She deflects that by saying the curse will be on her (27:12). Incidentally, it is not even clear what that means. Does she have the power to move Isaac's curse from Jacob onto her? With what authority? Commentaries (e.g., Rashbam, Chizkuni) interpret it to mean that *there will be no curse*, because Rebecca prophetically knows that the covenant will go to Jacob. Others (e.g., Ibn Ezra) explain that it is on her to get the curse removed.

Her drive does not stop there. After preparing the food, she dresses up Jacob to have a physical appearance similar to Esau's (27:15–16).

The plot succeeds. Jacob gets the blessings. Esau is furious and plans to kill Jacob. Again, Rebecca steps in to actively drive events. She tells Jacob to go to Charan to escape Esau's fury (27:43–45). Rebecca adds an additional tactic. She plants a seed with Isaac that perhaps he would like to encourage Jacob to find a wife who is not from Canaan (27:46). Once Jacob hears it from both parents, he complies (28:7).

We see Rebecca's defining role in driving events in the lives of Isaac and Jacob.

The Matriarchs demonstrate exquisite intuition on how to ensure that their children are protected and mentored properly. Sarah knew when Ishmael needed to be banished to protect Isaac (21:10). In her case, it was her own intuition – rather than guidance from God (although in the end, God agreed with her [21:12]). When the Torah says that Isaac took Rebecca into Sarah's tent (24:67), it is being more than figurative. Rebecca followed Sarah's path with equal intensity.

Indeed, in Rebecca's case, it is more than her intuition. From the very beginning, God informs her that Jacob is the chosen one. Rebecca's task is a greater personal challenge than Sarah's – both Jacob and Esau are Rebecca's children. She must favor one child over another. But she does what is necessary. While Sarah appears in some of Abraham's stories – often as a passive participant – Rebecca appears in almost every story and is a major driver of events.

Chapter 10

The Third Generation – Jacob

There are three generations of Patriarchs and Matriarchs. The ten tests that were applied to Abraham – and in some degree to Sarah – established that they had the qualifications required to be the progenitors of the Chosen People. They led exemplary lives in which they did all that was possible to qualify.

But it was not entirely in their hands. They didn't control their descendants. How would we ever know if they did enough? We *still* don't know if success will be guaranteed for thousands of generations! It seems that God wanted to see some multigenerational success. So God required that they demonstrate success of transmission to the next generation.

Hence Isaac – and to some degree Rebecca – was tested as well. Isaac did not have a full battery of tests. His first test was Abraham's final exam. He started the regimen by being subjected to an extremely challenging test – his binding at the altar. Once he successfully navigated that test, what remained was a single lifelong test to transmit the Torah to his offspring.

Isaac is successful at his tests. With Jacob, Isaac demonstrates that he too, is a successful transmitter of the Torah.

That brings us to Jacob. A full discussion of Jacob's life (Genesis (28–50) is beyond the scope of this book, but in keeping with our focus on the qualifications to be progenitors of the Chosen People, we will point to vignettes in Jacob's life that relate to that topic.

Jacob's Uneasiness

We discussed in chapter 8 how God had communicated his commitment to Jacob in Genesis chapter 28. While the message has been communicated to Jacob, he is not sure that he heard it as an unqualified commitment. This uncertainty will dog Jacob throughout his life.

We see the uncertainty in Rashi's interpretation of 28:22. Rashi explains that Jacob's oath of commitment to God in 28:20–21 is conditional. Jacob is saying that *if* God indeed meant the commitments as Jacob understood them, then all is fine. Even though Jacob thought he heard God make the commitments in 28:15, he is still unsure.

What is bringing about this nervousness? While it is not clear from the text, could it be related to the interdependence with Esau's blessing – the fact that there is a potential path in which Jacob may sin, while Esau has dropped the yoke (as discussed in chapter 8)? We will see a pattern that affects the rest of Jacob's life.

Or perhaps it was the language of God's blessing to Jacob that caused Jacob's nervousness. One of the most important parts of Abraham's blessing is that his descendants will inherit the gates of their enemies (22:17). When it is time for God to pass that commitment to Isaac (26:3), God is explicit. That which He promised to Abraham will be fulfilled through Isaac. And when Isaac blessed Jacob, he was equally explicit (28:4). He blessed him that God would transmit the blessing of Abraham to Jacob, including all the blessings that had been given to Abraham (such as the commitment of overcoming enemies).

God blesses Jacob as he is leaving Canaan with many wonderful things. The land will go to Jacob's descendants. They will be numerous and expand to the four corners of the world. They will be a blessing. God will watch over Jacob and return him to Canaan. These are terrific blessings. But significantly, they do not encompass the complete set of blessings given to Abraham. The conquest over enemies is missing.

Aside from Rashi's interpretation of 28:15, we also see the uncertainty in Ramban's interpretation of 28:12. In Jacob's dream, he sees angels ascending and descending a ladder to heaven. As part of a long discussion in one of his explanations, Ramban says that Jacob was shown the angels of four great empires ascending and descending. This was intended as an encouraging message – there may be times when Israel is conquered, but the conquerors will always descend. But there was one exception. The angel of Esau (Rome) never descended. Jacob asks what this means. He is comforted when God points him to the book of Ovadiah, in which there is a prophecy about the downfall of Esau.

In the context of the rivalry with Esau, all of this mixed messaging is significant. Isaac's model of the world was that there would be space for Esau, especially if Jacob sinned. Did the omission in God's blessing of dominion over enemies – together with Isaac's blessing that Esau *could* ascend with Jacob's descent – contribute to Jacob's life-long nervousness? Is the space that exists in the descending angels for the possible ascension of Esau something that Jacob needs to be concerned with? Let's look at that nervousness.

Jacob Encounters Esau

After building his family in Aram, Jacob returns to Canaan. His messengers tell him that Esau is approaching with four hundred men. Jacob is concerned (32:8). Why should he be? God had promised that "your seed shall be as the dust of the earth" (28:14). Jacob interpreted that to mean that all of his sons were included in the covenant – indeed, we know historically that was the case. God Himself had commanded Jacob to return to Canaan (31:3).

One might also wonder about Jacob's solution. He divides his family into two so that if Esau successfully destroys half of Jacob's camp, the other half can escape. This might be a sensible military strategy – hedging whether Esau will be friendly or not. But given that God had communicated that *all* of Jacob's seed were included in the covenant, it seems contradictory to worry that half could be wiped out.

Chizkuni, quoting the Midrash, explains the source of Jacob's fear. Jacob had been away from Isaac for twenty years. For twenty years, he had not fulfilled the obligation of respecting his parents. Perhaps such a sin was so awful that it could give Esau the upper hand, especially because Esau was so close to Isaac.

This explanation at first glance seems problematic. Jacob's departure from his parents was not a careless action by a runaway son. It was actually the fulfillment of a direct command from Isaac (28:2) to go to Aram and find a wife. It was also a direct command by his mother Rebecca (27:43) to leave until Esau's anger dissipated. Why should he be concerned about not respecting his parents while he was engaged in fulfilling their direct commands?

And in the same breath in which Jacob was commanded to leave Isaac, Isaac had blessed Jacob with the blessing of Abraham, to give Canaan to Jacob and his descendants (28:4). Moreover, why would Jacob expect to lose Divine Providence when God had just commanded him (31:13) to return?

Moreover, Jacob was not even expected back home. Rebecca instructs Jacob to leave until Esau's anger passes, at which point, "then I will send, and fetch you from there" (27:45). But that instruction never happened. So what was there for Jacob to fear? (Rashi 35:8 seems to indicate a Midrash that Rebecca did send for Jacob, but that was later.)

With our deeper understanding of the relationships between Isaac, Jacob, and Esau, we can better understand Jacob's fear.

Jacob had been away from his parents for thirty-four years. The first fourteen were spent studying with Ever (Rashi 28:9). The Talmud (*Megillah* 16b) derives from these fourteen years that the study of Torah is more important than honoring one's parents. But maybe what was obvious to the Talmud in retrospect was not yet known to Jacob prospectively. These were followed by the twenty years that the Torah reports his sojourn in Aram. He was away longer than necessary.

Jacob knew that his blessing was interrelated with Esau's blessing. Esau had been blessed by his father that if Jacob were to fall, Esau could remove Jacob's yoke.

Jacob understood the close tie between Isaac and Esau. He understood that Isaac would never give up on his attempts to bring Esau onto the right path. He also knew that Esau could be somewhat responsive. He was probably aware that Esau had taken a non-Canaanite wife (28:9), the daughter of Ishmael, and Ishmael had repented his own failings (Rashi 25:9).

This explains why Chizkuni specifies that Jacob was worried he had not sufficiently honored his parents. Jacob was not worried about other potential sins. He was not worried that some trickery in his business dealings with Laban would cause a problem. The mention of respecting one's parents is deliberate.

Showing respect to Isaac was Esau's best quality. What had happened in the subsequent thirty-four years? Had Esau continued to show respect? Did he repent as his half uncle Ishmael had repented? Was he now worthy as well?

And who would decide whether Esau had repented sufficiently? After all, in crafting the blessings, Isaac had said that when Jacob sinned, Esau would remove the yoke from his shoulders. Sure, Jacob had followed his parents' dictates. But how would that compare to a reformed Esau who was superlative in this one mitzvah? In other words, was Jacob's level of observance sinful relative to the bar set by Esau? And if so, could that jeopardize the blessing and the Divine Providence?

There are layers of irony to the respect that Esau had for Isaac. If not for that respect, perhaps Jacob would already be dead!

After the blessings went to Jacob, Esau hated his brother and declared that he would kill him once their father Isaac died (27:41). Rashi wonders why Esau would wait – why does he not kill Jacob immediately? Rashi explains that Esau did not want to upset his father. He was willing to have patience in his existential fight with Jacob out of respect for his father.

We said that Jacob *thought* he heard that all of his children would be in the covenant. But he was not absolutely sure. Taken together, there was enough cause for concern. His fear might have been irrational, since God had commanded him to return to Canaan. Nonetheless, a nagging worry continued to haunt Jacob.

And, at least according to some of our Sages, it was not irrational at all. In chapter 8, we already discussed the Midrash that Jacob was punished for hiding Dina from Esau. It seems that Dina might have had the power to straighten Esau out. If that could still happen, perhaps Jacob had a legitimate concern that he could be punished for withholding her.

Jacob and the Angel

One of the most difficult passages in the Torah is the story of Jacob fighting with the angel (32:25–33). Jacob encounters an angel and fights him all night long. In the morning, the angel wants to be released, which Jacob does only when the angel blesses him. Since the angel injures Jacob's thigh in the battle, the Torah reports that Jacob's descendants shall not ever eat from the sinew of the thigh vein of any animal.

What a strange story! Who was this angel? What does it mean for a man to have a physical battle with a noncorporeal angel? What does it mean for Jacob to win the battle? If God endowed the angel with a physical form, it is God who allowed Jacob to win. What was the purpose of the entire story? Why does Jacob's injury in a mysterious battle cause all descendants to refrain from a type of food – what is the connection?

The commentaries describe this vignette in relation to Jacob, Esau, and the blessings. In verse 25, Rashi tells us that the angel is Esau's guardian angel.

That sets the stage. The battle with the angel is a metaphorical battle with Esau. Radak takes it a step further. This encounter was to strengthen Jacob and build his confidence that he could survive the physical encounter with Esau without fear. This is an echo of what we described above – that Jacob was concerned whether he was still ascendant. Rashbam and Chizkuni take it a step further. Jacob was so fearful that he considered running away to escape Esau. The angel detained Jacob to ensure that he would see that God would protect him from Esau. In short, the encounter with the angel is a test of Jacob's perseverance.

Radak (32:26) makes a strong case for how Jacob was unnecessarily cautious. He starts by saying that Jacob was concerned that he had lost his immunity from Esau due to sins. Radak is explicit: after several promises from God, Jacob should not have acted so obsequiously to Esau. He was flattering him, sending presents, bowing to him – and he was punished for this.

These traditional explanations get greater resonance with the picture we are painting. The issues were not limited to whether Jacob would survive the physical battle with Esau. They related to Jacob's fears. His entire blessing, his entire legacy was interlocked by Isaac with Esau's behavior. He did not have clarity whether there could be an existential threat to the entire Chosen People project if Esau were to be deemed worthy at this point.

If the metaphoric battle arose from Jacob's insecurity about his blessings, then the metaphoric result was to strengthen Jacob's confidence that the blessings were indeed his and that God continued to be with him. This was accomplished in two ways. In a physical sense, the angel could not win the battle. As described by Chizkuni (32:26), the angel understood that God's purpose was to strengthen Jacob, so the angel had no permission to emerge victorious.

But the more relevant victory is when Jacob informs the angel that he will not release the angel without the blessing (32:27). Rashi's explanation is that Jacob was insisting that Esau's guardian angel admit (presumably on behalf of Esau) that the blessings rightfully belong to Jacob. Rashi sees that Esau was renouncing rights to the blessings received by Jacob as the main purpose of this battle. Again this is reinforced by how we have explained the centrality of the blessings.

That brings us to Jacob's injury by the angel. Radak, in critiquing Jacob, sees this as a punishment for Jacob having doubts. But Ramban relates the injury to our theme of the interplay between Esau and Jacob.

Ramban, quoting the Midrash, explains that Jacob suffers this injury for a particular reason. In the future, the righteous descendants of Jacob will suffer at the hands of Esau's descendants. While Jacob's victory over Esau's angel was a signal of Jacob's ascendancy, the injury was a reminder of the other part of Isaac's interlocking blessings. There is the possibility of a fall from grace when Jacob sins, and when that happens, Esau can be ascendant. With this explanation, the battle with the angel is a reproduction both of God's continued commitment to Jacob and of the caution introduced by Isaac.

With this understanding, we can explain why Jacob's descendants accepted a limitation on eating the sinew of an animal for the rest of time. The limitation is a reminder of the battle, which in turn is a constant reminder of the loftiness and responsibility of being part of the Chosen People. Jacob has the potential to be in covenant with God, as illustrated by most of the story. When he follows the correct path, Jacob is ascendant. But the responsibility is that Jacob must always believe in Divine Providence, be obedient of God's laws, and pass on the tradition. Otherwise, Jacob could be injured by Esau and lose dominion.

After the Angel

With the victory over the angel, Jacob is assured that the legacy of the Abrahamic dynasty will be channeled through him. Nonetheless, the concerns continue to arise throughout Jacob's life about his worthiness and the extent of God's covenant. Our purpose is not to go into Genesis chapters 32–50 in depth, but we'll touch on key instances in which Jacob's nervousness reappears even after the encounter with the angel.

The first vignette is stunning.

Jacob has his encounter with Esau. The story is well known. He offers many gifts to appease Esau. Esau seems appeased and suggests that they unite and go together. Jacob convinces Esau that there was reason to separate. It appears they have reconciled. Life is good.

There is one verse in this encounter that is breathtaking. Talking about the gifts, Jacob says, "Take, I pray you, my gift that is brought to you" (33:11).

The English word *gift* used in this translation is innocuous enough. But in the original Hebrew of the Bible, that is not the word that Jacob uses. Rather, he uses the word *birchati*; he is literally saying, "Take my blessing."

Indeed, classic commentaries interpret the word *birchati* in this context to mean gift. So the translations are correct. But we also need to look at the word that Jacob actually used, which reveals an incredible context.

Jacob and Esau have spent their entire lives in bitter battles about the blessings. At the age of thirteen, Jacob buys the birthright from Esau, which gives him some rights to these blessings. At age sixty-three, Jacob connives to get the blessings, leaving Esau so enraged that he wants to kill his brother. Twenty years later, one must assume that the anger might still be there – after all, Rebecca has not yet contacted Jacob to tell him to come home.

What is Jacob thinking in the usage of this word? Even if the meaning of *birchati* in context is "gift," why is he using the one word that has the greatest potential to set Esau off? Whatever Jacob means by the usage of this word, isn't he opening himself up to a great danger that Esau will try to kill him with this reminder?

Jacob must have used this word deliberately. Probably, he understood Esau's psychology better than anyone else.

When Esau was willing to sell his birthright to Jacob, he exclaimed, "Behold, I am at the point to die; and what profit shall the birthright do to me?" (25:32). In chapter 7, we quoted how Chizkuni interpreted the verse. Esau reasoned that since people do not live forever, the birthright and any benefits thereof are transient. Getting the Promised Land after his death was not worth much to him. Owning the birthright was not worthwhile in his eyes, because he was only concerned about his immediate livelihood.

When we consider the blessings given by Isaac to Jacob and Esau, *we* think about the meaning of those blessings for eternity. Which brother will ultimately be ascendant? Indeed, that is how Isaac and Jacob thought about the blessings. But arguably, Esau never thought about the blessings in those eternal terms, since his focus was on man's mortality. He was upset about not getting the blessings. But he was not upset about the eternal existential loss. He was simply upset about not getting the best fruit of the land or having the upper hand over his brother during his lifetime.

That was the genius of Jacob's appeasing Esau. He understood that if he formally kowtowed to Esau, he would give Esau the impression that Esau was ascendant, fulfilling "be lord over your brethren" (27:29). By giving Esau a substantial gift, he would fulfill "God give you…of the fat places of the earth" (27:28). Once the gifts were given, Jacob communicated that Esau received – in temporal terms – all that he ever wanted to get from these blessings. So he could say to his brother, *Here, I am giving you the blessing that I received from our father – you can stop hating me.*

Indeed, we recall that Jacob had received two blessings from Isaac. The first, originally intended for Esau, was the blessing that related to material goods. That was the one that Esau coveted, and that is the reason that Jacob's gift was an incredible amount of material goods (32:15–16). But in no way did Jacob try to appease Esau with the "blessing of Abraham." That was too valuable to Jacob, and it was unimportant to Esau.

There is a further irony in Jacob's statement that Esau should take the blessing. The immediately preceding vignette is the encounter between Jacob and the angel. As we described above, Rashi's interpretation of that encounter was that Esau was renouncing his claim on Isaac's blessing. Jacob originally legitimately got everything (the birthright and the blessing), but there was still a litigant (Esau) who was contesting this in some sense. Once Esau renounced the claims, it all belonged to Jacob without any disputants, so there was then nothing wrong with saying "take the blessing." Still, it would be quite insensitive to finally attain the full blessing (through the fight with Esau's angel) and then parade that fact to Esau the next morning. So more likely, Jacob was trying to assuage Esau's ego by providing him with the physical gifts and representing them as a suitable substitute for the actual blessings.

In the next vignette, in Genesis chapter 34, Shechem defiles Jacob's daughter Dina, and Shimon and Levi avenge her honor by destroying the city. Jacob's reaction (34:30) is to worry that the Canaanites will gather to destroy Jacob's family. We don't see a confident Jacob certain that he has God-given protection to emerge unscathed. Radak pointedly explains that Jacob was fearful, but his sons were brave.

In Genesis chapter 35, Reuven sins with Bilhah, but the Torah testifies that Jacob still had twelve sons (35:22). Ramban explains that this testimony teaches that Jacob did not disinherit Reuven for this sin. The constituency of the Patriarchs was finalized with Jacob. Once Isaac had completed the demonstration of transmission to his son Jacob, the subsequent generations were all part of the covenant. Jacob overcame any concern that transmission was limited to only some of his descendants.

Further echoes of the concern about "transmission to all descendants" appear in the story of the selling of Joseph. In Genesis chapter 37, Joseph's brothers sell him and dip Joseph's coat of many colors in blood. When Jacob sees the blood, he concludes that Joseph has died. The grief of a father for a lost son – especially his favorite son – is understandable. Jacob says, "I will go down to the grave to my son mourning" (37:35); as the Torah tells us, he refuses to be comforted.

But Rashi takes it to the next level. Rashi says that Jacob is not only grieving for his apparently dead son. He is also feeling sorry for himself. It is not only that Jacob will go to his grave in mourning. The word used for "grave" can also mean Gehinnom. God had previously told Jacob that if no son predeceased him, Jacob would not go to Gehinnom. What an unusual thing to think about when you've lost your son – is a father concerned about his own fate rather than his son's?

Jacob's concern about the personal impact can only make sense if it is part of a larger picture. The larger picture, always in Jacob's focus, is that all of his children were promised to be in the covenant. At the physical level, Joseph's apparent death was the loss of a child. But there was an existential point as well: Has Jacob lost the right to lead the Chosen People?

Verse 35 concludes with "And his father wept for him." Rashi brings from the Midrash that "father" in that sentence is a reference to Isaac. Isaac wept for the travail that his son Jacob was going through. Isn't it odd that the Midrash is bringing Isaac into the picture? Isaac literally has nothing to do with this story!

But Isaac's relevance is strong if we realize that this is part of Jacob's existential crisis. Isaac knew that Jacob's raison d'être was to be the one who delivers twelve tribes – all of the sons would be part of the Chosen People. Isaac also knew that Jacob was nervous about achieving this – partly because of Isaac's own blessings to his sons. That is why he needed to be brought into this story. He uniquely sympathized with Jacob's discontent because it ultimately was caused by Isaac's blessings.

Twenty-two years later, Jacob has not arisen from his tailspin. There is a famine in Canaan, and he sends his sons to Egypt. He holds Benjamin back (42:4), fearing an accident. He still lacks complete confidence about the survival of his remaining sons. When the ten remaining sons go to Egypt and Simeon is detained, Jacob is reluctant to send Benjamin despite the command of the ruler of Egypt (42:36). He continues to worry about his own destiny (42:38).

Ultimately, he has no choice but to allow Benjamin to go to Egypt. But he is in total despair. As he says farewell to his children, he says in desperation, "if I be bereaved of my children, I am bereaved" (43:14). The same Jacob who received all the blessings from Isaac – including the promises of the blessings of Abraham – is in a totally hopeless state.

The return to confidence takes place when Joseph reveals himself to the brothers, and they tell Jacob that Joseph is alive. Finally, at age 130, Jacob sees that the covenant indeed will rest on his whole family, and the Torah exclaims that Jacob's life returns to him (45:27). And in Genesis chapter 49, he brings the whole family together for his final message. There is no competition for who gets called in for which blessing, as there had been with Esau and Jacob. The Chosen People are complete. The sons have different roles and missions, but they are called in as a collective – as the sons of Jacob (49:2).

Takeaways

This book addressed the Torah's purpose in the vignettes in the middle chapters of Genesis. We pointed out the opinion of Rabbi Yitzchok that the entire Genesis (and some of Exodus) was primarily to demonstrate God's authority over the world, which supports God's decision to deed the Land of Israel to the Jewish people.

Indeed, Genesis chapters 12–28 accomplish that objective. First, chapters 1–11 demonstrated that God is the Creator and can destroy the world (in a deluge) at will. Those chapters proved God's authority and abilities. Chapters 12–28 communicate God's decision very explicitly that the Chosen People inherit the Land of Israel, emphasizing this quite a number of times.

We took it one level deeper. While the high-level objective that Rabbi Yitzchok sought is achieved, that could have been accomplished with much less text. This book searched for the purpose in having so much text to support this simple assertion. We explained the next level down: there were other important objectives. The Torah needed to explain why the Chosen People qualified to get this reward. We have seen the qualifications of obedience, belief, and dedication to transmission. After explaining the qualifications, the Torah explained how the Patriarchs and Matriarchs were tested for those qualifications.

The Torah's messages are never mere history lessons. It is interesting to understand retrospectively what the qualifications of the Patriarchs were. But if those are taught by the Torah, they must have an importance for every generation.

The simplest takeaway is that these qualities are expected from the Chosen People for eternity. God gave the Jews 613 mitzvot, and He expects obedience. He expects us to believe, and He expects us to transmit that belief.

We explained that "belief" is broader than the simple belief in God's existence. God has a purpose for the world, He cares about the world, and He is involved in the world. There is an expectation that the Chosen People have that broader belief about God. God has a purpose for the world, implying that we need to lead lives of purpose. That is elevating. It means that what we do and how we behave matters. Our behavior has cosmic and eternal importance. Armed with that understanding, we must take our every action seriously and carefully. Absent the belief that the world has purpose and our actions matter, we are reduced to being automatons whose own gratification may be the only purpose for being. Fortunately, there is more to life than that.

Transmission is the ingredient that has kept the Jewish people together. The Jewish people, like many peoples of antiquity, were a relatively small group. Through centuries of assimilation, conquest, conversion, and persecution, Jews and other people alike had challenges to their identities and culture. Many ancient cultures perished, but Judaism evolved and survived. One reason for Judaism's survival is God's watchful protection. But it is undeniable that fealty to the Jewish religion and the intense focus on transmitting it to the next generation played a major role as well.

If belief, obedience, and transmission have been the formula for millennia, it is worthwhile to reflect on those criteria in modern times.

In Western society, norms about traditional values are replaced by a cultural theme that people can do whatever they want, as long as it does not hurt others. This undermines obedience to God's everlasting norms. Western culture *does* accept obedience to norms that have currency. But norms imposed by a Deity prohibiting activities that don't obviously hurt others are *not* accepted in the modern world. Today's attitude is that it is difficult to sustain God's laws about forbidden relationships, forbidden foods and mixtures, and other restrictions. Sabbath restrictions are viewed as unnecessary curbs, rather than being viewed as a means toward holiness.

Social media spread this cultural theme with breakneck speed. Humans have a strong inclination toward a permissive attitude. If a cultural milieu indoctrinates our youth with permissive attitudes, maintaining traditional obedience has obstacles. Recognition that the Torah insists on obedience helps reinforce us against such cultural challenges.

Belief in Divine Providence can suffer a similar fate. We live in a hyperrational scientific society that tends to accept what can be proved and de-emphasizes opinions that aren't supported by hard evidence. Making decisions based on science is quite proper for topics within the domain of science. But science does not always teach values. And science is not able to peer into the unverifiable spiritual realm of religion. That makes it hard to introduce God into the public square. God has introduced Himself into our consciousness through prophecy and revelation at Sinai. But that was a long time ago. As discussed in *Genesis: A Torah for All Nations*, God cannot be in constant revelation to mankind if He is to preserve free will. Modern man has replaced fear of God with support of secular humanism.

None of the above is meant to minimize science or humanism. Science is the right approach for areas that lend themselves to scientific inquiry. And fundamental rights such as those expressed in the United Nations Declaration of Human Rights speak to real and valuable ethical norms. But science and humanist values don't address everything. They don't address God's definition of what society needs. Unfortunately, secular culture squeezes God and sanctity out of the discussion. Recognition that the Torah insists on belief helps ensure that we embrace God's values-oriented imperative for society.

In the same manner, transmission of the values – the third required quality of the Chosen People – is increasingly difficult. In the small communities that dominated throughout time, there was a natural advantage for parents or teachers to express their views and values unchallenged. By the time the next generation went out into the world, they were fortified with a lifelong attachment to the values of their ancestors.

Today, youth is raised in an open society, fingertips away from any idea imaginable. There is a high degree of exposure to different ideas, adding to the challenges of transmission. Even worse, there is a youth culture that is anti-authority and often anti-religion from the outset. Transmission is hard.

The messages of Genesis must strengthen our resolve to achieve the mission of the Chosen People nonetheless.

What are the consequences of failure? What if we simply ignore God's values and role in the world and rely on our own sense of right and wrong?

There are aspects of secular humanism that anyone can appreciate. There is a great deal of progress when society is based on secular values compared to the authoritarian values of corrupt leaders.

But by ignoring God's literal word, secular humanists exchange God's absolute standards for relative ones. Relative standards can invite immoral behavior or cheapen the value of life. In the extreme, a world with relative standards can be reduced to a world of no standards. How often have we seen authoritarian leaders co-opt the language of democracy for their own ends? The Chosen People have a unique responsibility to be role models of God's path. If they fail, that is Esau's invitation to ascend. In Esau's world, there can be a deceptive veneer of moral behavior. But if it is not backed by God's will, it ultimately may be undermined.

These modern challenges to achieving the ideals of the Chosen People are not necessarily more difficult than what the Patriarchs and Matriarchs needed to achieve. A subtext of Genesis is how difficult it has always been to achieve what God is asking from the Chosen People. In Abraham's case, he was barraged with ten very difficult tests. Isaac was nearly sacrificed at the altar and then had to deal with the challenge of Esau. Jacob lived through a bitter set of struggles (47:9).

Yet they overcame the challenges. The Torah may be telling us that we must believe, obey, and transmit. But the Torah is also telling us that it is difficult, yet we can overcome the challenges. We are learning what we must do – and that *we can do it.*

This primary message also has subsidiary messages. The Patriarchs – the focus of the text – did not do this alone and could not do this alone. The Matriarchs played a critical role – whether it was Sarah's higher level of prophecy or Rebecca's clearer understanding of destiny. Being "chosen" is not an individual mission – it is the mission of a family, a clan, a broad community that works together with common values.

And the lessons of Genesis 12–28 are not limited to lessons for the Jewish people. Genesis describes the world before and after the Jewish people were chosen. God cares about all the people on the planet. If the Jews were chosen, it was not to respect them to the exclusion of others. Rather, it was to provide a distinctive framework for greater commitment to God's will as a role model of what God expects from everyone on the planet – an ethical existence and fulfillment of God's expectations.

Appendix 1

Analysis of the Vignettes

In our introduction, we speculated about the characteristics that made Abraham and Sarah worthy to be the progenitors of the Chosen People. We first hypothesized that the Torah should describe their lives in glowing terms, outlining their outstanding positive attributes. But then we observed that in the text of the Torah are many vignettes in which their behavior was actually questionable. This appendix provides that detailed analysis.

We are looking at these stories through a modern lens. Perhaps in previous generations, these stories were not viewed as problematic. Perhaps in different times and in different cultures, readers would have viewed these stories more favorably. Indeed, reading the stories through the lens of the Midrash (which interprets many stories positively) is helpful. But it would have been more natural for the Torah to tell the stories in a clearly positive light.

This question deepens when one considers Rabbi Yitzchok's point, also discussed in the introduction, that there was no a priori need for the Torah to tell *any* of these stories. The point of the Torah is to teach mitzvot, a project that begins in Exodus chapter 12. He concludes that the only purpose of Genesis is to show God's greatness and His authority to have a covenant with Abraham. But if this section of the Torah helps us appreciate God's wisdom in choosing Abraham, then the logic should be clear.

To support this question, we partition the Torah's treatment of Abraham into thirty stories about him and assess whether at face value they represent heroic behavior: **Bold** stories are generally positive, negative stories are *italicized*.

As noted below, some of the negative stories have positive elements and some of the positive stories have negative elements. But this analysis supports the overarching conclusion that the Torah must have a different purpose than merely showing Abraham's heroics.

Vignette #	Verses	Vignette	Analysis	+/-/0
1	11:27–31	Abraham is born and later migrates with his family to Charan.	Abraham role was passive.	Neutral
2	12:1–3	God reveals himself to Abraham.	Abraham must be worthy, but his role in the story itself is passive.	Neutral
3	**12:4–9**	**Abraham follows God's directive to go to Canaan and tour many parts of the land; he then expresses gratitude to God.**	**Abraham's actions are laudable, but hardly heroic: How hard is it to follow God's direct commandment and thank Him?**	**Positive**
4	*12:10–20*	*During a famine, Abraham and Sarah go to Egypt. To save himself and to enrich himself, Abraham positions Sarah as his sister – not his wife.*	*Why doesn't Abraham just avoid Egypt? Why not be honest and accept the consequences as Abraham reportedly did when he was thrown into the fiery furnace (Rashi 11:28)?*	*Negative*
5	*13:1–13*	*Abraham's shepherds and Lot's shepherds have an altercation. Abraham recommends that they separate. Lot chooses to go to the evil city of Sodom.*	*Abraham's behavior seems questionable. Lot is a close relative – Abraham's nephew and Sarah's brother. True, there was an altercation. But was that enough reason to separate? What kind of family support is this? Lot took the arduous journey with Abraham from Charan to Canaan. Where was the family loyalty? Didn't Abraham see that Lot was going to Sodom? Couldn't he propose a compromise to prevent Lot from ending up in the evil city of Sodom?*	*Negative*
6	13:14–18	God repeats his promises to Abraham, who builds an altar.	While it must be positive that Abraham deserves these promises, there is no description of positive behavior other than the expression of gratitude through the altar.	Neutral

Vignette #	Verses	Vignette	Analysis	+/-/0
7	14:1–17	Abraham achieves a great military victory, rescuing the kings of oppressed cities.	This is complicated. The military victory itself is just a military victory – nothing of ethical content. Abraham is allied with the evil cities of Sodom and Gomorrah – a questionable set of partners. It may be positive that he retrieved the goods of his allies for them – or it may be questionable, given that the allies are evil.	Neutral
8	14:18–20	Abraham is blessed by Malkizedek.	This is mostly an unexplained blessing of Abraham, except that Abraham does tithe to the worthy Malkizedek.	Marginally positive
9	14:21–24	Abraham divides the spoils of war with the king of Sodom.	Abraham does not want to give the evil king of Sodom credit for enriching Abraham. (This one is actually somewhat questionable, because the result is the enrichment of the evil king.)	Positive
10	15:1–6	God tells Abraham that He will defend Abraham and Abraham will be rewarded.	Most of this is God bestowing promises to Abraham (for unspecified reasons), but there are two segments that are positive. First, God characterizes his blessing as a "reward," which indicates that Abraham was somewhat worthy; also, verse 6 is explicit that Abraham believed in God, which God counted as righteousness.	Marginally Positive

Vignette #	Verses	Vignette	Analysis	+/-/0
11	15:7–21	God enters into a treaty with Abraham to give him the land of Canaan and an expanse beyond.	Abraham is mostly passive in the dialog.	Neutral
12	16:1–3	Sarah asks Abraham to have children through her maidservant Hagar.	Abraham is neutral – following Sarah's instructions. Sarah is marginally positive, as she is trying to help Abraham.	Neutral
13	*16:4–16*	*Hagar becomes pregnant and despises Sarah; in response, Sarah oppresses Hagar with Abraham's tacit approval. An angel tells Hagar to endure the treatment and blesses her, but gives a report that Ishmael will be wild. Ishmael is born.*	*Abraham and Sarah's behaviors are highly questionable. Hagar's belittling of Sarah was uncalled for, but one would have expected a more enlightened response than harsh repression resulting in Hagar's fleeing the scene.*	*Negative*
14	17:1–22	God makes promises to Abraham (he will be the progenitor of many nations, a covenant, numerous descendants), changes his name from Abram to Abraham, and makes various demands (walk before God, circumcision).	Abraham is mostly passive.	Neutral
15	**17:23–27**	**Abraham and all of his household undergo circumcision.**	**Circumcision can be painful – but it's not surprising that Abraham would do it under direct command of God.**	**Positive**
16	**18:1–8**	**Abraham is hospitable to three wanderers.**		**Positive**
17	*18:9–15*	*Abraham and Sarah hear the news that they will have a son, Isaac.*	*Abraham is neutral. Sarah is so negative that she laughs in disbelief and then denies it.*	*Somewhat negative*

Vignette #	Verses	Vignette	Analysis	+/-/0
18	18:16–19	Abraham escorts the messengers toward Sodom, and God reflects that Abraham will command his family in the way of God.		Positive
19	18:20–33	God reveals His plans to destroy Sodom, and Abraham begs to save the city if there are sufficient righteous people.		Positive
20	Chap. 19	God destroys Sodom.	Abraham has a minor observer role.	Neutral
21	*Chap. 20*	*Abraham goes to Gerar and again tells the locals that Sarah is his sister.*	*Highly questionable, as above with Pharaoh.*	*Negative*
22	21:1–8	Isaac is born.	Abraham performs the circumcision and has a big party when Isaac is weaned. Like any other Jewish father. Nothing heroic.	Mostly neutral
23	21:9–21	Ishmael behaves badly to Isaac, so Abraham and Sarah send him and Hagar off with God's acquiescence.	This one is confusing. Sarah appears to be cruel – to the extent that her behavior troubles Abraham – yet God Himself says she is correct. Abraham appears compassionate to Ishmael, yet when he sends Hagar and Ishmael away, he provides few provisions – Hagar thinks that Ishmael will die (21:16). It is hard to call Abraham and Sarah heroic.	On balance, neutral
24	21:22–34	Abraham makes a treaty with Abimelech.	Seems mostly secular, except that at the end, Abraham calls in the name of God.	Neutral

Vignette #	Verses	Vignette	Analysis	+/-/0
25	*22:1–19*	*Abraham conducts the binding of Isaac.*	*This vignette is highly questionable. The Torah treats it as a positive story – based on Abraham's actions, God rewards him with many blessings (22:16–18). Yet Abraham is a Noahide. He knows he is not allowed to take a human life, but is apparently ready to do so.*	*Negative*
26	22:20–24	The genealogy of Rebecca is described.		Neutral
27	**Chap. 23**	**Abraham does a yeoman's job eulogizing Sarah, respectfully acquiring burial grounds, and burying her.**		**Positive**
28	*Chap. 24*	*Abraham dispatches his servant to go to his birthplace to find a wife for Isaac.*	*The Torah seems to view positively the fact that Abraham would only accept a daughter-in-law from his ancestral lands. In a modern view, this is hard to understand. According to our Sages, Abraham's family were idolators, and his retinue in Canaan included many people whom he and Sarah converted to Judaism. What was the great importance of not accepting one of these converts?*	*Marginally negative*
29	*25:1–6*	*Abraham remarries, has additional children, and sends them away.*	*Why send away one's children?*	*Negative*
30	25:7–10	Abraham dies.		Neutral

Let's take stock. Abraham lives 175 years. During those years, he has many relationships with parents, siblings, children, grandchildren, more distant relatives, and numerous kings and personas of the land.

I tried to rate the thirty stories as either positive, neutral/passive or negative/questionable. The results are:

- 9 were positive (3, 8, 9, 10, 15, 16, 18, 19, 27)
- 8 were negative (4, 5, 13, 17, 21, 25, 28, 29)
- 13 were neutral/passive (1, 2, 6, 7, 11, 12, 14, 20, 22, 23, 24, 26, 30)

When all is said and done, we should assume that Abraham was a great, righteous, and heroic individual, and all the stories are positive – however, it is not always clearly understood from the text. But the fact that it is not clearly understood is the actual problem. The key dilemma we are dealing with is to understand why the Torah chooses to characterize this hero's long life with a collection of stories – half of which are only neutral, approximately a quarter of which are superficially negative, and only about a quarter of which seem positive. And even the positive ones are often marginally positive – we are not seeing great, praiseworthy deeds. If the entire purpose of Genesis is to inform us how God rewards great people with covenants, why would the text not emphasize the worthiness of the recipient of the covenant?

Some say that Abraham's special virtue is his loving-kindness. Why don't we have thirty vignettes of his loving-kindness?

This then is the detailed analysis that supports the questions of the introduction that are addressed throughout the book. In particular, chapters 1 and 2 address these questions by pointing out that the detailed vignettes were required to show the qualifications and testing required for the Chosen People.

The Ladder of Tests and Blessings

In chapter 2, we discussed the interleaving of the tests and the higher levels of blessings/covenants as tests were passed. This appendix provides a tabular view of this.

Test Number	Verses	Content of Test	
Test 1 is given to Abraham	12:1	Depart Charan to move to Canaan **(obedience)**	

Blessing Number	Verses	Content of Blessings	Possible Interpretation
Blessing 1	12:2–3	• A great nation • Be blessed • Bless those who bless Abraham • Curse those who curse Abraham • Bless all people through Abraham	By sacrificing (leaving his homeland), Abraham gets personal greatness.

Abraham passes test 1	12:5		
Blessing 2	12:7	Descendants will get Canaan	A further reward having passed a test
Test 2	12:10	Famine **(belief)**	
Test 3	12:15	Taking of Sarah to Pharoah **(transmission)**	

Blessing 3	13:14–17	• Abraham and descendants will get Canaan as far as Abraham can see. • The gift of the land is forever. • Abraham's seed will be as numerous as the dust of the land.	Now that Abraham has passed the first set of three tests, there is a commitment to Abraham and his descendants forever. Hence they are a Chosen People. Since the second test included an exile (Egypt), there is a strengthening of the promise of the land. Since his family suffered, the promise of descendants is strengthened.

Test 4	Chapter 14	Battle of four kings versus five **(belief)**

Blessing 4	Chapter 15	• Abraham merits the higher form of daytime prophecy (Ramban 15:1). • God will defend Abraham. • Abraham will be inherited by his child. • Descendants will be as numerous as the stars. • The promise of Canaan is formalized via a covenant. • After a period of slavery, Abraham's descendants will accumulate great wealth. • The borders to be inherited will extend from the River of Egypt to the River of Persia.	The passing of the inheritance to Abraham's child is in distinction to Shem, whose children are not worthy. The covenant related to the land is strengthened after Abraham shows good custodianship of the land in the battle of the nine kings.

Test 5	16:3	Abraham's taking of Hagar **(transmission)**
Test 6	17:10	Circumcision **(obedience)**

| Blessing 5 | Chapter 17 (promised to Abraham prior to the circumcision – if he in fact does the circumcision) | • "13 covenants"
• Abraham will be the father of numerous nations.
• Abraham's descendants will be made numerous.
• God offers an everlasting covenant.
• God will be the God of Abraham's descendants.
• Canaan will be deeded to Abraham's descendants forever.
• Sarah will be blessed with a son.
• Nations will come from Sarah.
• God offers an everlasting covenant with Isaac.
• Ishmael will also be great. | By passing the second set of three sets, Abraham has twice shown himself worthy in the areas of **obedience, belief, and transmission**. While the testing will continue, he climbs another rung in the ladder. There is now a guarantee of an everlasting covenant through his child with Sarah. God and the descendants of Abraham are forever tied together. |
| Blessing 6 | 18:18 | • Abraham will be a great, strong nation.
• All nations will be blessed through Abraham. | Seems to be an additional blessing. |

Test 7	20:2	The king of Gerar takes Sarah (**transmission**).
Test 8	21:12	God commands Abraham to send away Hagar (**obedience**).
Test 9	21:12	Ishmael is expelled (**belief**).
Test 10	22	The binding of Isaac takes place (**belief, obedience, and transmission**).

| Blessing 7 | 22: 17–18 | • Abraham will be blessed.
• His descendants will be as numerous as the stars and dust.
• His descendants will conquer enemies.
• All nations will be blessed by his descendants.
• The language of all of these blessings is in the form of an "oath" from God. | The completion of the ten tests raises Abraham to the highest level as he is confirmed as the Patriarch of the Chosen People. Two main things are added, both related to descendants. Descendants figure prominently here because the blessings are now less about Abraham as an individual and more about the Chosen People that will result. The first is that the descendants will conquer enemies. The second and most important is that the descendants are blessings (and also role models) for all people of the world. Additionally, as the Ramban explains, these guarantees are raised to the higher level of an oath from God. (Hirsch explains that the previous guarantees were given with a "covenant" – i.e., each side must fulfill its part of the agreement. With the binding of Isaac, Abraham had kept his agreement, so now it was a one-way oath from God.) |

Appendix 3

Explanation of Key Vignettes

In appendix 1, we described how there were several vignettes that appeared to put Abraham and Sarah in a questionable light. In some cases, we have also asked why there were discussions in the Torah that seem irrelevant to the main purpose of the Torah. It was important to explain the circumstances better to appreciate why the actions were justified. The table below summarizes the key points of chapter 5, by elaborating on a subset of the chart from appendix 1.

Vignette #	Verses	Vignette	Analysis	+/-/0	Explanation
4	12:10–20	During a famine, Abraham and Sarah go to Egypt. To save himself and to enrich himself, Abraham positions Sarah as his sister – not his wife.	Why doesn't Abraham just avoid Egypt? Why not be honest with Pharaoh and accept the consequences as Abraham reportedly did when he was thrown into the fiery furnace (cf. Rashi 11:28)?	Negative	chapter 5

Vignette #	Verses	Vignette	Analysis	+/-/0	Explanation
5	*13:1–13*	*Abraham's shepherds and Lot's shepherds have an altercation. Abraham recommends that they separate. Lot chooses to go to the evil city of Sodom.*	*Abraham's behavior seems questionable. Lot is a close relative – Abraham's nephew and Sarah's brother. True, there was an altercation. But was that enough reason to separate? What kind of family support is this? Lot took the arduous journey with Abraham from Charan to Canaan. Where was the family loyalty? Didn't Abraham see that Lot was going to Sodom? Couldn't he propose a compromise to prevent Lot from ending up in the evil city of Sodom?*	*Negative*	*Chapter 5*
7	14:1–17	Abraham achieves a great military victory, rescuing the kings of oppressed cities.	This is complicated. The military victory itself is just a military victory without ethical context. Abraham is allied with the evil cities of Sodom and Gomorrah – a questionable set of partners. It may be positive that he retrieved the goods of his allies for them – or it may be questionable given that the allies are evil. There is also a larger question of what the purpose of this vignette is in the Torah.	Neutral	Chapters 4 and 5

Vignette #	Verses	Vignette	Analysis	+/-/0	Explanation
13	*16:4–16*	*Hagar becomes pregnant, despises Sarah, and in response Sarah oppresses Hagar with Abraham's tacit approval. An angel tells Hagar to endure the treatment, blesses Hagar, but gives a report that Ishmael will be wild. Ishmael is born.*	*Abraham and Sarah's behaviors are highly questionable. Hagar's belittling of Sarah was uncalled for, but one would have expected a more enlightened response than harsh repression resulting in Hagar's fleeing the scene.*	*Negative*	*Chapter 5*
21	*Chap. 20*	*Abraham goes to Gerar and again tells the locals that Sarah is his sister.*	*Highly questionable, as above in vignette 4 with Pharaoh.*	*Negative*	*Chapter 5*
23	*21:9–21*	Ishmael behaves badly to Isaac, so Abraham and Sarah send him and Hagar off with God's acquiescence.	This one is confusing. Sarah appears to be cruel – to the extent that her behavior troubles Abraham – yet God Himself says she is correct. Abraham appears compassionate to Ishmael, yet when he sends Hagar and Ishmael away, he provides few provisions – Hagar thinks that Ishmael will die (21:16). It is hard to call Abraham and Sarah heroic.	On balance, neutral	Chapter 5

Vignette #	Verses	Vignette	Analysis	+/-/0	Explanation
25	22:1–19	Abraham conducts the binding of Isaac.	This vignette is highly questionable. The Torah treats it as a positive story – based on Abraham's actions, God rewards him with many blessings (22: 16–18). Yet Abraham is a Noahide. He knows he is not allowed to take a human life, but is apparently ready to do so.	Negative	Chapter 5
28	Chap. 24	Abraham dispatches his servant to go to his birthplace to find a wife for Isaac.	The Torah seems to view positively the fact that Abraham would only accept a daughter-in-law from his ancestral lands. In a modern view, this is hard to understand. According to our Sages, Abraham's family were idolators, and his retinue in Canaan included many people whom he and Sarah converted to Judaism. What was the great importance of not accepting one of these converts?	Marginally negative	Chapter 5
29	25:1–6	Abraham remarries, has additional children, and sends them away.	Why send away one's children?	Negative	Chapter 5